"The church has a key role in su
mental-health difficulties. To d
ical services means that the ch
much, for we are not competing, but not *nothing*, for there are past errors of over-spiritualising we can learn from. This book delivers just the right amount and then wraps it in a biblical model to integrate this with our faith and enable real change. Helpful indeed!"

Dr Rob Waller FRCPsych, Consultant Psychiatrist; Founding Director, The Mind and Soul Foundation

"What a brilliant resource! The authors bring compassion, intelligence, biblical wisdom and practical help to bear on this most difficult of topics. Combining exceptional clarity of thought with real-life examples, they empower readers to offer genuine Christian hope and help to those struggling with mental-health challenges."

Dr John Burns, Head of Counselling Services, Shore School, North Sydney, Australia

"Steve and Helen have achieved the seemingly impossible task of taking a complex issue and framing it for a local-church audience. This book brims with a helpful distillation of mental health—terms, definitions, explanations—while also presenting the beauty and depth of the gospel. Readers will be educated, encouraged, equipped and edified for the privilege of caring for souls."

Jonathan Holmes, Pastor of Counseling, Parkside Church, USA

"As one who has suffered with my own mental health in recent years, I am utterly delighted that Helen and Steve have written this book. It's all that I hoped it would be and much more! Full of wisdom, warmth, compassion and practical help, it left me full of hope. I will be encouraging every church member to get hold of a copy."

Andrea Trevenna, Minister for Women, St Nicholas Church, Sevenoaks, UK

"I am so grateful for this outstanding and timely book. Every church will benefit from reading it in book groups, as individuals and in pastoral teams. The writing is warm, soaked in grace and informed by years of caring, listening and loving. The content is intensely and realistically practical. I look forward to reading it again and learning to put it into practice."
Christopher Ash, Writer-in-Residence, Tyndale House, Cambridge

"Without sidestepping the important roles of mental-healthcare professionals and medications, the authors highlight, through worked examples, what the church can and should do to become a welcoming, wise, Christ-like community for strugglers."
Michael R. Emlet, Dean of Faculty, CCEF;
Author, *Saints, Sufferers and Sinners*

"Instructive, compassionate, encouraging and informative. This is a timely, significant and much-needed book for church members and church leaders. Awareness of our own mental health is growing, and some struggle more than others with the severity of mental illness. This book highlights that we are in the struggle together."
Elinor Magowan, Director of Women's Ministry, FIEC, UK

"I have had mental-health problems for a long time and have sat with countless others who do too. I found this a really helpful book and would strongly encourage pastors and those in pastorally supportive roles in churches to read it."
Julian Hardyman, Senior Pastor, Eden Baptist Church, Cambridge, UK

"I wish I had had this vital and timely book 30 years ago; I'm glad I have it now. It's easy to read, insightful in content and thoughtful in application. It's especially encouraging to read how a healthy local church community can be a help and blessing to those in need and that the approaches needed are within reach of every Spirit-filled believer. Helen and Steve's book is now on my 'essential reading' list."
Adrian Reynolds, Head of National Ministries, FIEC, UK

MENTAL HEALTH
AND YOUR
CHURCH

A Handbook for Biblical Care

Helen Thorne and
Dr Steve Midgley

Mental Health and Your Church:
A Handbook for Biblical Care
© Helen Thorne and Steve Midgley, 2023.

Published by:
The Good Book Company

thegoodbook.com | thegoodbook.co.uk
thegoodbook.com.au | thegoodbook.co.nz | thegoodbook.co.in

Unless indicated, all Scripture references are taken from the Holy Bible, New International Version. Copyright © 2011 Biblica, Inc. Used by permission.

A CIP catalogue record for this book is available from the British Library.

ISBN: 9781784987787 | Printed in Turkey

Design by Ben Woodcraft

CONTENTS

CHAPTER 1

LIFE IN THE LOCAL CHURCH

The local church is a messy place. But it doesn't always look that way.

Sometimes we can walk into church and get the impression that everyone is fine. But many are not. Behind the bright smiles and buzz of conversation, they are struggling with something hard. It's one of the consequences of the fall—that moment recorded in Genesis 3 when humanity decided to stop living God's way. Since then, we've all had bodies that don't quite work as they should, hearts that go astray and minds that are broken in one way or another. Since the fall, we've all experienced hurtful things and had to live with the legacy of that pain.

For some, that hardship is relatively manageable: a little stress, an occasional worry, a few aches and pains—nothing that requires a medical diagnosis or any sustained pastoral support. For others, however, the pain of life runs deep; they are dealing long-term with the fallout from serious illness or the lingering consequences of deep relational hurt. For some of our brothers and sisters in Christ, life can be dominated by struggles of the mind: long-term battles with thoughts, feelings, impulses and even voices that distract, drag down and nudge them towards despair.

As you cast your mind around the congregation of which you are part, maybe you can think of people who are struggling now—people who have shared their pain with you and, possibly, asked for help. Maybe, with sadness, you can remember those who used to come but have drifted away—people you tried to get alongside but who didn't stay. Undoubtedly, there will be people whose hardships you don't know about. Battles with mental ill-health are often kept deep inside.

People you may know

Maybe you know people like these:

- **Chi** has been a Christian for as long as she can remember. She loves Jesus deeply and wants to serve him with all of her life. Every Sunday she's at the service and every Wednesday she attends her small group, but she rarely says a word. It's not that she doesn't love people. It's not that she has nothing to contribute to discussions about God's word. She's just scared. Chi is utterly paralysed by a fear of getting things wrong or saying something that may upset someone else in the room. At night, she battles panic attacks. Gastrointestinal challenges blight her day. And frequently she cries. Life feels so very hopeless—she just doesn't want to be this way.

- **Andy** is young, single, intelligent and doing well in his career. Normally, he's the life and soul of the Bible-study group—always cracking jokes, offering to help or organising social events. But things haven't seemed quite right in recent months. It's been a gradual thing, but he and a couple of people around him have been noticing that he has less energy, less enthusiasm and a kind of gloominess that just isn't like him. Despite having many friends, Andy feels increasingly alone. A natural self-confidence is giving way to darker thoughts about being a failure and having let everyone down. The early mornings are the worst.

Sleep is elusive, and lying in the darkness, he can genuinely believe he's unlovable and without value, and that the world would be a better place without him. His thoughts get very bleak then, and a cursory glance at his tablet search history would show that he has recently begun to explore how people go about ending their lives.

- Possibly you know someone like **Siobhan**—an occasional attender at church, at best. Her life is chaotic, marred by abuse past and present, the pain of which she dampens with whatever she can afford. Every day there's alcohol; her flat is littered with empty bottles and the cheap corner-shop bags in which they came. Some days there's cash for drugs—cannabis or occasionally heroin if she's been able to beg, borrow or even steal from family or friends. When she's sober, she loves reading God's word and praying. There have been so many times when she's tried to get clean. But the bottle always seems to trump the Bible in the end. Most people gave up on her long ago.

- Every now and then we meet a **Ben**. He's been ill since his early 20s—which is when the voices began and his grip on reality started to drain away. His parents remain supportive, and he usually joins them at church, but at times it's been extraordinarily difficult. When his psychotic symptoms are acute, Ben's convinced that he's Jesus—reincarnated and with new revelations to share. Even when things are calmer, he still struggles to order his thoughts and to locate himself reliably in reality. Medication helps, but it has side effects, and these make him reluctant to take it. He finds it hard to sit still. So often you can see him pacing at the back of the service; he wanders out for a cigarette before coming back in. Ben sometimes attends a small group but expressing himself is difficult. He either dominates with inappropriate expressions of his delusional beliefs or sits looking distracted as if his thoughts are elsewhere. People want to love him, but they just don't know how to.

• Or how about **Kelly**? She's a lovely, godly woman. She's gifted, humble, kind—just the sort of person you want reading the Bible one to one with the younger women in the church. But she's struggling at home as her youngest teenage daughter seems to be disappearing before her eyes. She doesn't understand why her daughter isn't eating; she can't get her head around the cuts on her daughter's arms. This time last year the family were so happy: mealtimes were a joy, and feelings were shared and not suppressed. But something somewhere broke. Now she feels impotent in the face of her daughter's slow-motion self-destruction. And nothing, either from friends or anyone else, even begins to help.

There are plenty of other stories we could include here. Stories of people with phobias, personality disorders, obsessions and flashbacks—those riding the bipolar roller coaster from mania to despair and back again or those quietly wondering "Am I going mad?" because of the unexpected impulses they are feeling. Statistics tell us that, worldwide, one in six of us will have experienced a mental-health struggle in the past week. Globally, serious depression is the second leading cause of disability.[1] This is reality. And here is the first thing we need to grasp. Mental unwellness is not the rare exception—this is normality for every church.

---

1 Source: www.mentalhealth.org.uk/statistics/mental-health-statistics-uk-and-worldwide (accessed 11 August 2022).

Mental illness is hard

Having mental-health struggles is a difficult pain to bear. Everyone's story is unique, but there can be some common threads among all who know its scourge. There are the very real burdens of the negative thoughts, heightened (or muted) emotions and impulses that need battling day after day. Decision-making can feel impossible and relating to others as complex as having to communicate in a foreign tongue. From the challenge of getting out of bed in the morning to the near impossibility of focusing on the tasks in hand, through to not being able to sleep when so much in your mind is going astray, the simple act of living can feel unendingly hard.

There can be challenges with medication too. Prescription drugs can be helpful in many ways—indeed sometimes they are essential for safe functioning in life—but they often come with side effects that just don't feel "right". It can be hard to stick to the medication when it means that you don't quite feel like yourself any more.

But, more than any of those medical considerations, there's something about mental illness that feels isolating—othering: it seems to mark people out as being different, and few people want to be apart from the crowd. It's so common to be, or at least to feel, misunderstood.

In recent years, great strides have been made in the Western world to promote understanding and empathy for those with mental-health issues—to bring it out of the closet. But there can still be stigma attached to mental illness. Words like "crazy", "psycho" or "mad" may be intended light-heartedly, but they often wound deeply. Many countries have legislation in place to ensure that people with mental-health struggles are not unfairly disadvantaged in the workplace. But often sufferers find it hard to be open about their battles for fear that it will end any prospects of promotion, or simply make their colleagues view them differently or doubt their capability to do their job well.

Even in the local church, there can be a reluctance to share out of fear of being ostracised or seen as someone whose faith is weak. People will rally round a congregation member with cancer far more quickly and easily than someone whose diagnosis relates to the mind. Mental illness is perceived as confusing, weird, something that only specialists should engage with and, potentially, too long-term for any sustainable care.

Sadly, many whose mental-health struggles have been made public have been on the receiving end of words that, while well-intentioned, simply make things worse. It's not hard to find people who have been falsely accused of being manipulative, lazy, making a fuss, causing a scene, or just not having enough faith to see them through. There's still a sense that they ought to be able to "snap out of it" or pull themselves together. Most would if they could. If only change could happen that simply or in that short a time.

But even when the outer voices are helpful, as they genuinely can be in many local churches, there is often an inner voice that whispers to the Christian, "If you really believed in Jesus properly, you wouldn't be like this". "Christianity is meant to be a faith of joy, peace, self-control, and victory, isn't it? So why are you feeling like this?" Such thoughts often induce guilt. They encourage people to wonder how God views those whose minds are flooded with sadness, fear, impulsivity, and despair. They nudge Christians towards believing that their Lord and his people would really rather like it if they were somewhere else.

Walking alongside those with mental illness can be complex. But supporting people with mental-health struggles can be hard too.

Reasons why I can't get involved

You may never have known the hardship of not being able to string two thoughts together or hold on to what is right and true. If you haven't experienced such pain yourself, it can be genuinely difficult to understand what those who are struggling are going through.

When it comes to helping, it can also be tricky to know where to begin. Is it most appropriate to start with physical needs? There's often some shopping that could helpfully be done. Or should we advocate for the person in need to access services? Or listen to them as they talk about their pain? Maybe we should be opening Scripture with them—we are believers after all? How about praying? But what do ask God for? Are we praying for healing, for help, for hope?

Some of us have maybe tried helping people in the past and just found it exhausting. We don't want to go there again. The late-night and early-morning phone calls, the circular conversations, the arrangements to meet up that keep getting cancelled at the last minute and the seeming lack of change can bring us to our knees. It's not that we don't care, but we feel we just don't have the capacity to keep on caring as much as there seems to be need.

Maybe you have known the agony of losing someone close to addiction, anorexia or suicide. The pain is unspeakable; the grief hard to bear. We didn't manage to help last time, so what makes us think we could make a difference to someone else now? Not only can our confidence to help ebb away but, much more seriously, our confidence in the Lord can be hard to maintain: after all, if he really is sovereign and so good, why didn't he make things right? Why did it turn out so horribly?

It's not hard to find people who will tell us that mental illness is for specialists only. Indeed, most of us in churches will have only a rudimentary understanding of all the various biochemical, social and spiritual theories of mental illness there are. But often our reservations go deeper than that. Talk of faith will only confuse, we suspect. There are matters of safety to consider. An untrained helper might cause more harm than good. Only those with high levels of expertise should attempt to get involved, we're told—and when we're looking for an out, it's an appealing idea to hold on to.

For those in leadership there is the very real tension about how to deploy resources and time. There may be many sheep in our care—to what extent can we focus on the needs of the few? Will committing to help the few leave the many at greater risk than is fair? And, more fundamentally, what is our call? Is the biblical role of pastor-teacher one that encompasses care of the mentally unwell or should that high calling sit elsewhere?

Add in our own personal experiences of mental health and some of us can feel the pull to withdraw still more. Maybe we are so acutely aware of our own depression, anxiety or other struggles that we simply feel we have nothing to give—not right now anyway.

But despite the hardships of those struggling and the complexity for those trying to care, one thing is certain: when the local church is acting as a local church can, the results for all involved can be a delight and not a burden.

The local church can be beautiful

Come with me on a moment of imagination. Can you begin to envision a church like this?

- **A family** where brothers and sisters in Christ with mental-health struggles aren't just welcome but actively feel able to share openly without fear of judgment—where no one recoils from tales of depression, suicide or addiction, and lives are truly shared.

- **A body** where members genuinely empathise with one another on the good days and the bad—rejoicing with those who rejoice and weeping with those who weep.

- **A flock** where everyone's spiritual needs are provided for and everyone is given encouragement to keep following their Shepherd King, understanding that the needs of sheep are not "one size fits all". Some can walk; others need carrying. And that's ok.

- **A place** where all can use their gifts—even if they are struggling substantially—because we are convinced that every member of Christ's body is an essential part and, if supported appropriately, will be able to serve.

- **A fellowship** where resources are shared so that no one is in any physical need, and gifts are given with no thought of what we can get in return.

- **A community** where everyone is active in supporting others so that no one gets burned out by having to shoulder all the work.

- **A congregation** where everyone can be loved and safe; where gentle boundaries are in place that work for the good of all; where all can know the joy of being transformed to be more like Christ; and where perseverance is pursued and grace abounds on those inevitable days when everything goes horribly wrong.

- **A gathering** so countercultural in the way it treats people with mental-health struggles that the unbelieving world can't help but sit up, take note and ask "Who is the God whose followers act like this?"

Can you imagine a church like that? Can you imagine your church being like that? Is this a mere fantasy? A flighty obsession by someone who's been given one book contract too many?! Quite the opposite—it's what the Bible calls us to.

Our calling

Trawl through Paul's epistles, the letters of Peter, James and John, the narrative of Acts and the ministry of our Saviour himself (not to mention the centuries of believers faithfully living life in the Old Testament according to God's law) and we will see a consistent pattern emerge. The worshipping community is designed to be a place where all followers of Jesus can come and flourish in their faith—and where no one is excluded.

The abused, the broken, the ill, the deluded, those ground down and ostracised by the fallenness of life—*all* have a home in the church through Christ. The depressed Elijah, the abused Joseph, the raped Tamar, the fearful Moses, the desperate King David, the bitter Naomi, the Corinthian Christians who had come from a background of alcohol misuse, the woman at the well whose life was imploding in multiple ways—all were valued members of the worshipping community, at least in God's eyes. Those who struggle today don't have an invitation to belong merely as second-class citizens; the church is still designed to be a first-class home for everyone who puts their trust in Christ.

This side of heaven, we'll never get it completely right. The new heavens and the new earth will be such a joy when all of us have perfect bodies and minds, perfectly worshipping our perfect Saviour. But before that time, we'll all be limping a bit, and our churches will be imperfect in areas like this. But, as with so many aspects of the Christian life, we can begin to taste the beauty of the new creation now. In our local congregations, we can at least glimpse what it is for all Christians—those struggling with their mental health and those who aren't—to worship in Spirit and in truth, in unity, in love, in relationship, in service and in hope.

It's a call worth fighting for.

And that is our aim for the rest of the book: not to turn you into mental-health professionals but to equip you with knowledge and wisdom, and to help grow that attitude of love and compassion towards those who struggle. Only when we learn to reflect the compassion that Christ has for all of us will we be able to truly play our biblical role in welcoming, nurturing, growing, and labouring alongside those who struggle—for the glory of God and the good of those around.

But what exactly is mental illness, and what does the Bible say about it? It's there that we need to start.

Questions for reflection

1. What experiences have you had of struggling with your own mental illness? How did other Christians react to you? Did you feel you could tell them about your struggles?

2. Which of the reasons for *not* getting involved with those suffering from mental illness most resonate with you?

3. How do you think your church is currently doing in regard to helping those with mental-health struggles?

SECTION 1

UNDERSTANDING MENTAL ILLNESS

CHAPTER 2

WHAT'S IN A DIAGNOSIS?

In considering what the Bible has to say about mental health, an obvious place to start is with definitions. What exactly is mental illness? When we speak about "mental-health issues" or "psychiatric disorders", what is it that we mean?

The answers to such questions might, at first sight, seem relatively straightforward. We know what it is to be physically well, and we also know what being ill physically is like. So, if it is much the same with mental illness, then the boundary between health and illness should be clear. On Monday I was fit and well. Then on Tuesday I got the 'flu. Then a week later I was well again. I was healthy, but then I became sick. And then I got better again. *Simple*. On that basis there would be just two categories: some people are mentally healthy and others are mentally sick. Some people's minds are working normally, and some aren't. Only it just isn't like that. The boundaries are anything but simple.

Am I well, or am I sick?

In fact, when we stop to consider it, we discover that even the boundaries between physical illness and health aren't that clear either. In the case of an undiagnosed cancer, we might *feel* perfectly healthy and fit, even though we are, in reality, seriously and dangerously ill. Or we might have a long-term illness (like thyroid disease) that is being so well treated that we feel perfectly well, and there are no impacts on how we live our lives day by day. Does that mean we are still ill, or should we say that we are well again? Certain kinds of ill health, like hypertension (raised blood pressure), are largely unconnected with how we feel. We may feel fine, but, without treatment, the condition may create very serious illness in the future. Is that an illness or an illness waiting to happen?

With mental health, things are even more complicated. Not least because questions about normality and abnormality are much less clearly defined. Hypertension is recognised because there is an identifiable normal range, and research can predict the likelihood of long-term health problems with different levels of hypertension. But how does that work with mental illness? Can stress be defined on a statistical basis? If our stress level is above the "normal range", does that make us ill? But what if we are living in a war zone—wouldn't high levels of stress be expected? In fact, wouldn't the absence of stress be considered abnormal in such circumstances?

So, is this simply subjective? Should individuals decide for themselves whether they are mentally healthy or mentally ill? That might have some logic to it, but it would make mental illness very different to other forms of illness. So it seems we do need objective measures of our mental functioning. But how will those measures be established and by whom?

Many symptoms of mental illness are common to us all. We all know what it is to feel low in mood, and everyone gets anxious sometimes. But we don't consider this to be low-grade mental illness—we see it as part of normal life. Only when such experiences last a long time or recur frequently or increase in intensity, do medical terms begin to be used. Instead of "feeling a bit low" we speak of "being depressed" or even "having depression".

Circumstances matter too. A person who is feeling low and anxious might be living through a pandemic or might have been bereaved. That changes the significance we give to these "symptoms", because we know that life affects us. The presence of a reasonable "cause" changes the way we think about mental distress. Should it also change the language we use? Or is cause irrelevant to diagnosis?

Faced with these complexities, we may wonder how to proceed. This chapter has two aims. The first is to reset our thinking regarding psychiatric diagnoses so that we see them more as *descriptions* rather than *explanations*. Our second aim is to reduce the stigma felt by those struggling with mental illness, by showing how the problems experienced in this area have connections with all of us.

How do you feel about a spider in the bath?

We should notice, first, that the boundary between mental illness and mental health is not as sharp as we might usually think. Instead of black and white *categories*, we encounter *spectrums*.

Take, as an example, the anxiety we might feel about spiders. It varies widely. Some people, faced with a spider in the bathtub, will casually pick it up and pop it out of the window; others will do so only while holding a tissue; still others will use that well-established cup-and-card trick. Some will summon a friend and get them to remove the spider instead. Move further along this "fear of spiders" spectrum and we encounter someone who won't visit the insect house at the zoo or cannot enter their own garden shed. More troubled still is the person who has avoided their friend's house ever since they noticed cobwebs on the ceiling. At the very far end of the spectrum is a person so beset by a fear of spiders that they never leave their house. Stuck at home in protective clothing, their days are consumed with anxiety as they constantly renew the grout which fills every skirting board crack to keep the enemy out.

Many of us are scared of spiders, but for some that fear is profoundly disabling. The first is "normal"—even "perfectly healthy"; after all, if you live in Australia, your reaction to spiders is potentially a matter of life or death. The second is "abnormal": something we'd describe as "mental illness". But where, precisely, is the dividing line? At what point does normal fear become a spider phobia?

Many, if not most, of our struggles with mental health can be located on spectrums in this kind of way. Some people are trusting; others are wary. Some express concerns about increasing state control; others fear conspiracy. Where does legitimate caution become paranoia?

Our moods vary too. Some are upbeat; others are gloomy. Cups can be half full or half empty. In some, mood varies widely; others are more constant. Are such variations connected to mental-health issues, or are they some completely different phenomena? It's complicated.

Putting a name to a condition

Psychiatry (the branch of medicine that deals with mental illness) tries to clarify what is, and is not, mental illness by providing us with clear definitions. Diagnostic classifications offer objective and, where possible, measurable criteria that can define psychiatric disorders. The Diagnostic and Statistical Manual (DSM) is one such classification system, and its diagnostic criteria for a specific phobia (like a spider phobia) is set out below.

A. Marked fear or anxiety about a specific object or situation (e.g. flying, heights, animals, receiving an injection, seeing blood). (Note: In children, the fear or anxiety may be expressed by crying, tantrums, freezing or clinging.)
B. The phobic object or situation almost always provokes immediate fear or anxiety.

C. The phobic object or situation is actively avoided or endured with intense fear or anxiety.

D. The fear or anxiety is out of proportion to the actual danger posed by the specific object or situation and to the sociocultural context.

E. The fear, anxiety or avoidance is persistent, typically lasting for 6 months or more.

F. The fear, anxiety, or avoidance causes clinically significant distress or impairment in social, occupational, or other important areas of functioning.

G. The disturbance is not better explained by the symptoms of another mental disorder, including fear, anxiety, and avoidance of situations associated with panic-like symptoms or other incapacitating symptoms (as in agoraphobia); objects or situations related to obsessions (as in obsessive-compulsive disorder); reminders of traumatic events (as in post-traumatic stress disorder); separation from home or an attachment figure (as in separation anxiety disorder); or social situations (as in social anxiety disorder).

There are many positive elements to classifications like these. First, they seek to provide a reliable way of making a diagnosis. Two psychiatrists comparing their experiences in treating people with bipolar disorder or schizophrenia can have confidence that they are talking about the same kind of thing. Without such classifications we wouldn't know whether a study showing an effective new treatment really was a breakthrough or if, perhaps, the study had simply involved people with milder problems. Secondly, these classifications help us notice experiences that cluster together. Mania has many typical features, and its diagnostic description alerts us to features we might otherwise overlook.

Remember, though, that these definitions simply *describe*. They do not generally *explain* (although there are a few exceptions to this—for example certain forms of dementia). A diagnosis provides a label that we can use to name an experience—and that is a valuable thing to do—but understanding the causes of that experience and how it might be treated are a completely different matter.

In that sense psychiatric diagnoses are different to most other medical diagnoses. When a doctor says you have chicken pox or Type 1 diabetes, that diagnosis provides an explanation. Chicken pox is an infection caused by a particular virus (varicella-zoster, in case you're interested). Type 1 diabetes happens because of reduced insulin production from the pancreas, which leads to raised blood-sugar levels. In both cases the underlying causes (the "pathology") is understood.

But when a doctor says you have OCD (obsessive-compulsive disorder) or anorexia nervosa or bipolar disorder, what you have is a descriptive label. You can describe *what* is happening but not *why*. That is a key difference in almost all psychiatric diagnoses. And it matters because of what it implies (or doesn't imply) about our understanding of treatment and cure.

The scope of mental illness

Some people find getting a diagnosis a relief because it brings a kind of recognition of their experience. Increasingly, however, concern is being expressed, even by mental-health professionals, about the "medicalisation of human experience". Difficulties we might usually describe in non-medical terms have acquired psychiatric labels. Social Anxiety Disorder describes what most would think of as extreme shyness. Intermittent Explosive Disorder describes someone who can dramatically lose their temper.

Such experiences are, of course, profoundly problematic.

People troubled by these experiences deserve our care and attention. But it is worth asking whether the language of illness is helpful. Will providing a psychiatric label help make sense of a person's experience? Will it increase the likelihood that they will get the care they need?

A diagnosis may provide a measure of orientation in the face of troubling and confusing experiences. It may even spur us on to search for solutions. But, more often, getting a diagnosis (psychiatric or not) tends to move us in the direction of *passivity*—we become people to whom something is happening rather than having a strong sense of personal responsibility. Patients, typically, are passive. We submit to examination; we receive a diagnosis; we take a recommended treatment. In accepting expert opinion, we can lose a measure of our own capacity and responsibility. In some situations, willingness to acknowledge a problem and seek help can be tremendously important. But not always. Sometimes losing a sense of personal agency can contribute to our struggle rather than relieve it.

This short chapter can't do justice to the complex issues that surround the use of diagnostic labels. It can, however, at least highlight three initial implications.

1. The issue of continuity: *"I am part of this"*

Noticing the spectrums which apply to so many psychiatric conditions and mental-health struggles helps us to resist that unhelpful "us and them" attitude. If you have never received help from professional mental-health services, you may want to distance yourself from "those mentally-ill people". But this distinction is a pretence. We may be at different places on these spectrums, and others may struggle more than we do, but in all sorts of ways we are much more alike than different. Acknowledging this helps us identify with those struggles. It helps us connect.

As we consider ways in which our churches can respond in this area, this is so important to understand. Changing our thinking about labels and diagnoses helps us to resist the damaging stigma that exists. It helps us to be the body of Christ and move towards one another in love rather than away from each other in fear. We can empathise with those wrestling with their mental health because we see that their experiences are not so different from our own. Their anxiety may be off the scale, but we all know what worry is like. They may be overwhelmed by paranoid delusions, but we all know what it is to feel "got at"—and how we hate it when people seem to be ganging up on us. We can, in this sense, "normalise the abnormal" and help create bonds of love towards people who often feel so very alienated in church.

2. The issue of involvement: *"I can help!"*

Once we see mental-health issues in continuity with our experiences instead of distinct from them, we begin to see that we *can* have something to offer. We don't need to be scared of mental illness, as if it requires a kind of care that is entirely beyond us. That doesn't mean we won't value mental-health professionals. Their experience provides them with a familiarity with mental-health problems that others lack. They have skills which enable them to provide help and support in ways we probably can't.

And yet, that experience and skill are not exclusive to professionals. Making links with our own experiences helps us find points of connection. We know how physical activity—taking a walk, doing a jigsaw—helps us when we are feeling flat. We know how creating a plan helps in the face of anxiety. By recognising, in our own experience, the value of the healthy habits of eating, sleeping and exercise, we can apply the same things to the lives of others. We also know how much we appreciate people taking time to listen to us and understand the problems we are facing. Knowing this, we can offer that same gift of time and attention to others. The experiences others face may, initially, seem strange and hard to relate to. But by slowing down and reflecting on related experiences of our own, we can begin to identify what has helped us and gain confidence in offering support to others.

3. The issue of faith: *God speaks!*

The final shift we might notice when we stop thinking of psychiatric illness as totally alien to us is our appreciation of the way God speaks powerfully and repeatedly to address these experiences—because he understands the frailty of fallen humans and has deep compassion for us. What the Bible has to say to us about ordinary levels of fear will also be connected to what it says to those facing profound fear. Indeed, many of the Bible's narratives describe extreme peril and struggle and can speak into situations of profound need.

Scripture speaks about guilt and about hopelessness and about despair. It will require time and patience, and great care, if we are to speak comforting biblical truth into the guilt and hopelessness and despair of a profound depression, but it can be done. What we want to resist is the idea that mental-health disorders place people into such a distinct category that Scripture no longer has a voice there.

Questions for reflection

1. Where did you fit on the "spider scale" of anxiety? Do you know others who would put themselves at a different point on the scale?
2. How do you feel about the label of mental illness? Have you had the experience of pulling back from someone who has a diagnosis like this? Why?

3. What parts of the Bible have given you comfort and help when you have faced stress, anxiety or confusion? How might you share your experiences and the effect those truths had on you with others?

CHAPTER 3

DEVELOPING A BIBLICAL UNDERSTANDING OF MENTAL ILLNESS

We have already seen that defining mental health and mental illness is complicated. Trying to identify causes of mental illness is equally complex. But believers who struggle in this way, and those wanting to support them, do need a framework that helps make sense of these experiences. This chapter will provide some pointers toward developing a more biblical understanding of mental illness.

What "causes" mental illness?

Sometimes the cause of mental illness seems obvious. **Anne** was involved in a road traffic accident; **Bijan** witnessed a murder. Both developed acute anxiety and grew fearful of leaving the house. In each case, agoraphobia was diagnosed, and it would seem obvious that circumstances had caused this anxiety to develop.

Cindy has struggled with depression for a decade. So did her mother and her grandmother before that. It seems obvious to everyone that Cindy's depression is genetic.

Soo Jin developed low mood over the three months following the birth of her first child. Her family feel sure she is depressed because "her hormones are all over the place" after giving birth. Just the same thing happened five years previously when she went on the oral contraceptive pill. Then the low mood disappeared completely as soon as she stopped taking it.

Some things just seem obvious, as in the four examples above. But that doesn't always mean they are.

Matthew attributes his feelings of depression and guilt to his failings at work. As he readily admits, two serious errors of judgement on his part led to the firm making substantial financial losses. Several colleagues have lost their jobs as a result, and he is so plagued by guilt that he hasn't been able to face work for four months. It seems obvious that circumstances have triggered this depression… Only there *were* no errors of judgement. And no financial losses. And no job losses either. Matthew's depression has distorted his perception of what really happened. Sometimes what seems obvious isn't.

Many factors contribute to the development of mental illness—sometimes those factors can be identified, but more often they can't.

It also seems clear that social trends have a bearing on mental illness. The high incidence of eating disorders in the West strongly suggests that cultural factors have a bearing on causation. When women and, increasingly, men are bombarded by images of the perfect body shape, it seems obvious that this is contributing to the development of anorexia in women and bigorexia (properly known as muscle dysmorphia) in men, where they obsessively exercise to achieve that "shredded" look.

Does the cause really matter?

If we think of mental illness as purely a biological phenomenon, then identifying the cause may not seem to be very important. If depression is caused by changes in brain chemistry and remedied by medication, then all that matters is taking the right medication. Identifying the cause might not seem to matter. But few people take such an absolute stance.

Most recognise that traumatic events and prolonged stress and inadequate support networks can make mental-health problems more likely. Identifying and doing something about those factors will, therefore, be worthwhile.

Moreover, even if we can't identify a particular cause, we can still identify factors that may slow recovery or increase the likelihood that a mental illness will recur. For all these reasons we will want to develop a way of understanding mental illness that allows for the many different factors that seem to be involved. This will help us both with prevention and the provision of support.

As Christian believers, we will also want to consider the role that spiritual factors may have in relation to mental illness. It is vitally important that we avoid any suggestion that faith protects a person from becoming mentally ill. Some Christians seem to see mental illness as something that only happens to those whose faith is immature—as if a strong faith will prevent a person from ever becoming depressed.

Yet on the other hand, it would be odd if prayer and a trusting relationship with the Lord had nothing to offer someone struggling with their mental health. We believe these things will be helpful to someone facing a physical illness and the same must be true with a mental illness. To say that there are things we can do as believers to help ourselves when we are anxious or depressed isn't the same as saying that anxiety or depression was caused by spiritual weakness in the first place.

What we need is a model that incorporates all the varied factors that are operating in mental illness. To arrive at such a model, we must begin with some first principles to build a biblical understanding of who and what a human being really is.

Who do you think you are?

Who we truly are and what factors make us that way are questions about which the Bible has plenty to say. We are people who have been created by God and made in the image of God (Genesis 1:26). In the psalms people are both "fearfully and wonderfully made" (Psalm 139:14) and "sinful at birth" (Psalm 51:5). In Christ we are made a new creation (2 Corinthians 5:17), but we still battle the sinful nature (Galatians 5:16; Romans 7:21-23). These things all have a bearing on the way we understand the experience of mental illness in a believer.[2]

Your heart

The Bible uses many different words to describe the inner life of a person. Among them are "soul", "mind", "inner person" and "spirit". But the term "heart" probably most fully captures the biblical concept of the core of a person. Biblically, the heart is the moral, decision-making centre of a person. The heart determines the direction of life because it is with our heart that we form commitments and allegiances. Another way to describe the heart is as a kind of "worship centre". All of us have something that we make our greatest good—the goal towards which we strive. The Bible's language for that is *worship*. Whatever we believe is "worthy" to have the focus of our affections and the best of our energies is the thing that we worship. And it is with our heart that this worship happens.

Here are just a few examples of the way the Bible uses the language of "heart":

> *The word is very near you; it is in your mouth and in your heart so that you may obey it.*
>
> Deuteronomy 30:14

---

2 This scheme is based on ideas from Mike Emlet, "Understanding the Influences on the Human Heart", *Journal of Biblical Counseling* 20:2, 2002 (Winter 2002).

"Now then," said Joshua, "throw away the foreign gods that are among you and yield your hearts to the LORD, the God of Israel."   Joshua 24:23

I will give you a new heart and put a new spirit in you; I will remove from you your heart of stone and give you a heart of flesh.   Ezekiel 36:26

For where your treasure is, there your heart will be also.   Matthew 6:21

These people honour me with their lips, but their hearts are far from me.   Matthew 15:8

Since, then, you have been raised with Christ, set your hearts on things above, where Christ is, seated at the right hand of God.   Colossians 3:1

The key activities in our lives—the emotions we feel, the thoughts we think, the decisions we take—derive from our hearts. We would expect the things that we think and feel and decide to reflect our priorities. Or, to put it in biblical language, we would expect our thinking and feeling and decision-making to reflect our worship.

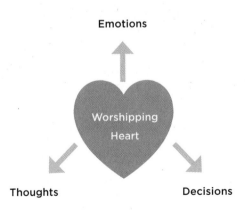

In considering people, we begin with the heart because the heart is central to our identity as creatures. But our hearts are affected by other aspects of human experience, not least our physical bodies.

Your body

God has made us physical beings—a part of the material world which God has made. Everything we do and everything we experience happens through the medium of our physical frame. We hear with physical ears, speak with physical mouths and touch using the physical surface of our skin. When we decide to walk, nerves send messages to muscles, and muscles contract. All our interactions happen through the medium of our physical bodies. When we think, it is reflected at a physical level by the neural activity of our brains.

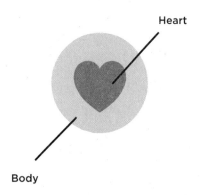

Heart

Body

Clearly what happens to our bodies affects us. We can see the profound way women are affected by the hormonal changes associated with their menstrual cycle. These changes don't just affect a woman physically; they make an impact on the whole of her. The same is true of physical illnesses and the side effects of medication and the influence of our genetic coding—all these things are bodily experiences and physical phenomena but they obviously affect all of us. A broken night's sleep, a bout of food poisoning, a cleft palate—all these physical things make an impact upon our thoughts, feelings and decision-making. Just being hot or hungry can be enough to make some of us irritable and irrational.

Moreover, the activity of our inner life also affects our bodies. When we are embarrassed, we blush. When we are anxious, our heart rate increases. When we are afraid, we can physically tremble. There is a two-way interaction between our inner lives and our bodies. What we believe and fear and rejoice in gets expressed in our bodies, but equally what we experience in our bodies impacts our thoughts.

In his list of trials and struggles in 2 Corinthians, Paul writes about his "hunger and thirst" and being "cold and naked". He recalls physical floggings and "a thorn in my flesh" (2 Corinthians 11:24-27; 12:7). Jesus experienced hunger and tiredness (Matthew 4:2; John 4:6). Physical experiences affect us and contribute to our mental well-being or our mental ill-health.

And there is still one more influence to be aware of.

Your world

Every person lives in a specific cultural and social moment. Living in the West in the 21st century is very different to living in Palestine in the 1st century. Sometimes those differences seem to create very different struggles, as with the body-image disorders we considered earlier. Other stresses are remarkably similar whatever culture we are living in. The social circumstances that surround us—our immediate friends and family, our wider social network and the culture of the place where we live—will inevitably affect us. The views, beliefs and expectations of our culture are bound to make an impact upon us.

For example, each family has its own set of cultural expectations and ways of doing things. Some families are strict and organised; others are more casual, perhaps even chaotic.

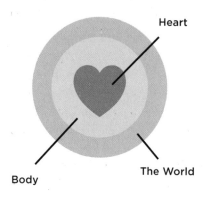

In the early 2020s we lived through a global Covid pandemic. That changed the way we related to others and the way we worked. Some people live through wars and others through natural disasters. These things all make a particular impact upon us.

The Bible knows this. Old Testament characters like Job describe the impact of hardship in this way:

> *Sighing has become my daily food;*
> *my groans pour out like water.*
> *What I feared has come upon me;*
> *what I dreaded has happened to me.*
> *I have no peace, no quietness;*
> *I have no rest, but only turmoil.*   Job 3:24-26

Job's immense losses impacted his emotions. A confident and joyful man was brought low.

We see the same thing in many places in the Bible. Losing

her husband and her two sons brought Naomi to a state of bitterness. David became fearful as he ran from the deranged Saul. Amos and Habakkuk speak with anger about the injustice they witness. Elijah despairs as he reflects on his isolation and the unfaithfulness of the community around him. Bad stuff happens, and it impacts our mental well-being.

The New Testament knows these things too. It describes scoffers (2 Peter 3:3), deceivers (2 John 1:7) and believer's personal hardships (2 Corinthians 1:8-9). Jesus himself experienced these things (Mark 5:40; John 8:55; 1 Peter 4:1). The Bible doesn't see faith as a kind of protective bubble rendering us immune to the effects of our fallen world. Paul, writing to the Corinthians, notes that…

> *We are hard pressed on every side, but not crushed; perplexed, but not in despair; persecuted, but not abandoned; struck down, but not destroyed.*
> 2 Corinthians 4:8-9

Faith makes a huge and significant difference, but Paul is still hard pressed, perplexed, persecuted and struck down. He still hurts! In fact, many of Paul's struggles were directly *caused* by his faith. The Bible often uses battle imagery to describe the Christian life (Ephesians 6:12; 2 Corinthians 10:4; 1 Timothy 6:12) and identifies a spiritual enemy, the evil one, who, Jesus tells us, is the father of lies (John 8:44). Precisely how the reality of spiritual warfare and the development of mental illness interact in any individual experience may not be at all easy to determine, but that such factors are at play is clear.

An understanding of mental health and mental illness that seeks to do justice to the Bible's understanding of people must make room for all these factors: our physical bodies, our cultural and personal circumstances and the activity of our hearts.

We should also recognise that surrounding these three elements there are broader spiritual realities at work. First and foremost there is the sovereign Lord, who rules over us and over all things and who will achieve his ultimate good purposes. But there is also a power for evil. And although God's victory over the evil one is certain, in the present age he can still bring damage and deception upon the people of God.

A worked example

Emma has been feeling low for six months: consistently flat and lacking in energy, waking early in the morning and with a low appetite. Emma will tell you that life feels empty and the future looks bleak. Nothing brings her pleasure or joy. Emma has many of the classic features of depression. But why has this happened? Why is Emma depressed?

A year ago her older brother died suddenly and unexpectedly from a brain haemorrhage. He was only 46. Emma and her brother were really close, and she misses him desperately. Two months after his death, Emma had her third miscarriage. This one was at 18 weeks, just when she was beginning to think the pregnancy was safe. She and her husband remain childless despite input from the local fertility clinic.

So perhaps this is what psychiatrists used to call a "reactive depression"—a response to circumstances. But there are other factors at play...

Emma has a family history of depression. Her mother has been depressed several times as has her twin sister. Emma also recently started taking some medication for high blood pressure. One of the side effects listed for the medication is low mood and depression. Perhaps, then, physical, biological and genetic factors are behind her depression. But that's still not the end of the story...

Five years ago, Emma had an affair. She hid it from her husband, who only found out when he saw an email message on her laptop. She was apologetic and said it was a kind of madness. She regretted it hugely, and with input from a counsellor at their church, they've begun to rebuild their marriage. But trust has been lost, and Emma feels deep guilt and shame. And even though her pastor and her friends at church remind her of God's grace, Emma wonders if God will really forgive her. She now constantly volunteers at church, hoping to gain more assurance. Those close to her, including her husband, say this is consistent with the perfectionist and controlling way she has dealt with so much in her life.

So why is Emma depressed? Is it because of her body, or her circumstances, or her heart? The question defies a simple answer. Lots of things are affecting Emma. It simply isn't possible to tease apart the interlocking strands apart and declare what is causing what.

But even if we could fully attribute Emma's depression to her recent bereavements, investing time in her spiritual health would still be worthwhile. Her mistaken beliefs about God and the gospel are important to address, whether or not they are a contributing factor in her depression.

And here is the point: we don't need to know that a spiritual issue is causative to decide that it is worth addressing. All of us have issues of the heart to deal with, and it is good for us, and glorifying to God, if we grow into a fuller and richer knowledge and love of God. That is true regardless of what impact such thinking may or may not be having.

The final cure for mental illness

The long list of troubles which have affected Emma (as well as the troubles she herself is responsible for creating) make us long for a time when such struggles will finally be at an end. And, according to the Bible, such a day is coming—a day when mental illness will be no more. But we won't see that day this side of the new creation.

The Bible never promises an end to struggle in the here and now. But when Jesus returns and ushers in a new heaven and a new earth, suffering will finally be at an end. And that includes the suffering and struggles from mental ill-health. On that day our relationship with Jesus will be fully restored. Our worship will no longer be distorted but fully and rightly focused on him. And with that will come a restoration of relationships with others as well. Our bodies will no longer be subject to decay. There will be no disorder to our biochemistry. No pain inflicted by others and no pain arising from our own unwise choices. And no physical or spiritual threats to deal with.

That will indeed be a good and glorious day—when all sickness and tears will, as Revelation 21 reminds us, be gone for ever. For those in Christ, that day is a certainty. We won't be struggling with mental illness for eternity—that's "just" for the here and now.

However, we don't have to wait until eternity for glimpses of that good. Churches that teach the gospel and whose communities reflect the grace of that gospel will be good for our mental health. And we need to explore some of the many ways that God can make a difference, not just in the future but also in the here and now.

Questions for reflection

1. Think about a time when you have struggled. What do you think the causes might have been?

2. How does it help our mental health to know that we are both gloriously made and fallen?

3. As you consider friends with mental-health problems (or your own struggles) how might it help to be aware of the impact of circumstances and body and heart?

CHAPTER 4

MEDICATION

Some introductory cautions

This is a short chapter about a big topic. The use of medication in mental illness has attracted lots of attention in recent years, and this will only scratch the surface. This is certainly not the place to look for detailed answers about specific drug treatments. Comments about individual drugs would, in any case, be out of date in no time because things change so quickly. This chapter offers some general principles to help chart a course in understanding the role of medication in mental illness.

Topping up your serotonin tank

Tanya had been struggling with low mood for some months. It was hard to get out of bed, hard to get to work, hard to get to small-group meetings. Things got so bad that she visited her doctor. He gave some helpful general advice and suggested they meet again in a couple of months. He said that, if things hadn't improved, it might be worth her starting some antidepressant medication and suggested she give that idea some thought. Not knowing much about antidepressants, Tanya asked advice from some close friends, and one of them, Sharon, said she had recently read a helpful article about this online.

According to Sharon, the article explained how there is a substance called serotonin, which is naturally made in our brains and that induces a sense of happiness and well-being.

We all have something like a "serotonin tank" in our brains, which needs sufficient quantities of this substance in it to keep our mood positive. Sometimes the tank gets too low, and when that happens, we experience depression. Taking an antidepressant changes that. SSRIs (Selective Serotonin Reuptake Inhibitors), the article said, work by topping up the tank and restoring the right level of serotonin. Once the level is restored, our mood improves, and the depression disappears. Tanya found this explanation hugely helpful not least because it made taking antidepressants seem so obviously the right thing to do. She went back to her doctor and started on antidepressants the following day. She said she was feeling positive about the future for the first time in months.

The description of depression that Tanya was given likens it to diabetes or an underactive thyroid. Someone with diabetes isn't producing enough insulin in their pancreas and needs insulin by injection. Those with an underactive thyroid have low thyroxine (the hormone produced by the thyroid gland) and need thyroxine supplements. In much the same way, this understanding suggests that depression is caused by a deficit of serotonin, which can be solved by antidepressants.

Only it just isn't that simple.

The complexity of the brain

Many years ago I (Steve) was taking a class in neuropharmacology—the study of drugs that work on the brain. The professor teaching the class made a striking comment that I've never forgotten. "What you need to understand," she said, "is that with our current understanding of brain functioning and with the drugs we have available, all our efforts to affect brain functioning with the use of drugs is a bit like a mechanic trying to mend a faulty car by opening the bonnet and hitting the engine with a hammer!" For a woman at the very forefront of her academic field to speak in such a way seemed both remarkably honest and remarkably humble.

Much research has been done since then. More brain chemicals have been identified and more brain receptors too. The complexity of the brain is only too clear. Understanding how it functions and how that functioning is related to mental illness is extraordinarily complex.

We can identify diabetes or an underactive thyroid by measuring the level of relevant hormones in the blood. The test confirms the diagnosis. But it doesn't work like that with depression. There is no blood test (or brain scan) that shows us the level of our serotonin. The idea that depression may, in some way, be connected with serotonin derives from studies which show how antidepressant drugs work. We can't directly measure serotonin in the way we can hormones in the bloodstream. There isn't a clear 'proof' of the serotonin theory of depression.

What is cause and what is effect?

What's more, even if we were able to prove that people who are depressed have low levels of serotonin, we'd still be left with a question relating to cause because we wouldn't know if we had found the chicken or the egg. In other words, are changes in our brain chemistry the cause of a low mood or the result? Of course, if you believe there is nothing more to us than our physical bodies—that we are simply a collection of cells and chemicals—then the chicken-and-egg question doesn't really matter. But most of us don't think like that.

When we smile or laugh or fall in love, things happen in our brains. The chemistry does something. But not many of us are ready to believe that falling in love is nothing more than a quirk of our brain chemistry. We take it that if there are changes in our brain chemistry, they are the result of falling in love and not the cause.

If we view depression in the same way, it prevents us from thinking that depression is due to just a "leaky" serotonin tank. That's important because it counters the passivity which leaves me thinking there is nothing I can do except wait for the tank to top up again. This doesn't mean that taking antidepressants is somehow wrong. Relieving the symptoms of a low mood can be important, and that is what antidepressants seem to do, even if we aren't quite sure how.

A brief history of drugs in psychiatry

It's striking just how many of the breakthroughs with psychoactive drugs (drugs which work on our brains) have been accidental. Chlorpromazine was the first drug to be widely used in the treatment of schizophrenia. It's efficacy was "discovered" when some antihistamine-like drugs were being tested in the treatment of a condition known as "post-surgical shock". Researchers noticed that the patients who took chlorpromazine were more relaxed about their surgery and needed fewer painkillers afterwards. That led them to wonder if it might be useful in psychiatric conditions. Its use from the 1950s onwards transformed the way in which psychiatrists managed people with severe mental illness.

In more recent history, the use of SSRIs has expanded considerably because studies have shown previously unexpected effects. Drugs originally used for depression are now used for anxiety and obsessive compulsive disorder and premenstrual symptoms. This isn't because we have learnt new things about the biological causes of these conditions but simply because such drugs seem to help.

Side effects and other difficulties

There are several examples in the history of psychiatry of times when drugs became extraordinarily popular only for problems to become apparent later on. Valium, otherwise known as diazepam, emerged in the 1960s as a treatment for anxiety and was soon being prescribed very widely. However, it became obvious that people were getting dependent on (addicted to) diazepam and were suffering very problematic withdrawal syndromes once the drug was stopped.

Much has been written about the iconic antidepressant drug Prozac (fluoxetine). There have been concerns expressed about side effects and an increasing awareness of the withdrawal symptoms that are associated with these SSRIs (the class of drugs to which Prozac belongs). Perhaps it is inevitable that any drug which affects the functioning of our brains (and remember how complex the brain is) will have both positive effects and effects we don't want.

Take it because it works

In *Mind Fixers,* Harvard professor Anne Harrington provides a comprehensive historical survey of what she describes as "psychiatry's troubled search for the biology of mental illness". In her conclusion she notes how psychiatrists from different eras have made "audacious promises on which they could not deliver",[3] producing a series of false dawns as psychiatry lurches from one preoccupation to another. At one time the solution was the asylum, then psychoanalysis, then surgery and electroconvulsive therapy (ECT), and then improved social conditions, and now it is pharmacology. The promotion of each new solution, she notes, always seems to be associated with the ridiculing of what has gone before.

It's clear that many factors contribute to the development of mental illness. It would not be surprising, therefore, if a range of treatment approaches would help. Rather than seeing drug treatments as the "one size fits all" solution on

---

3 Anne Harrington, *Mind Fixers: Psychiatry's Troubled Search for the Biology of Mental Illness* (W.W. Norton & Company, 2019).

the one hand or some kind of capitulation to non-Christian thinking on the other, we might be better served by seeing medication as one possible way of alleviating distressing symptoms, which will be useful for some people alongside other forms of support and help.

Some common groups of medication

Antidepressants: As the name suggests, these drugs seek to treat the low mood experienced by those who are depressed. There are many different types of antidepressants. Those most commonly used in the past were the tricyclics or MAOIs (Mono-Amine Oxidase Inhibitors). But, partly because they are safer when taken in an overdose, SSRIs are now more commonly prescribed. By stopping the reabsorption of serotonin, these drugs are assumed to increase the amount of serotonin available at neuronal junctions and this is the usual explanation for the way they affect mood.

As well as their use in depression, SSRIs are used in various anxiety disorders—including PTSD (Post-Traumatic Stress Disorder), social anxiety and OCD (Obsessive Compulsive Disorder). They are also used to help in situations that are less obviously psychiatric, like PMS (Premenstrual Syndrome, and with feelings of aggression.

Other newer antidepressants such as mirtazapine and venlafaxine seem to have effects on both serotonin and noradrenaline.

Side effects vary from drug to drug, but with SSRIs some of the more common side effects include nausea, reduced appetite (but sometimes increased appetite), headaches, sleep disturbances (either feeling sleepier or not sleeping as well) and some effects on sexual functioning.

Anxiolytics: These drugs reduce symptoms of anxiety. The benzodiazepines include drugs like diazepam (longer acting) and lorazepam (shorter acting). Their impact is thought to be via a neurotransmitter called GABA, which is believed to produce the calming effect. Because of their addictive properties, benzodiazepines are generally only used for short periods.

Various other drugs are also used to reduce anxiety—these include SSRIs, pregabalin, venlafaxine and buspirone.

Again, side effects vary from drug to drug. Benzodiazepines, for example, can cause confusion, sleepiness or problems with coordination and balance. Usually these can be managed by adjusting the dose.

Antipsychotics: These drugs, sometimes called "major tranquillizers", are used to treat people who have been diagnosed with more severe psychiatric disturbances, such as schizophrenia and paranoid states. They are used in acute situations as a treatment for people experiencing hallucinations and delusions, and also as a maintenance treatment to try and prevent psychotic symptoms from returning. Long-term treatment is sometimes given by a "depot" injection of a slow-release version of the drug.

The main theory explaining how these drugs work is that they block dopamine receptors in the brain. That is also associated with their side effects. Dopamine is involved in the control of muscle and movement, and these drugs can produce symptoms a bit like those of Parkinson's disease, such as stiffness and tremor.

Mood stabilizers: Some people get recurring episodes of depression or may alternate between episodes of depression and something called mania—a kind of overactive, grandiose state often associated with poor decision-making. Mood stabilisers are taken long term with the aim of preventing or at least reducing either the frequency or severity of such episodes. The drugs used here include lithium as well as some anti-epilepsy drugs like carbamazepine and sodium valproate.

Lithium can produce serious side effects when levels in the blood get too high, and people taking it are given regular blood tests to ensure they are getting the right dose. Weight gain, thyroid disorders and gastrointestinal symptoms are some of the common side effects. Some people find that taking lithium or other mood stabilisers leaves them feeling a little "flat".

Principles for using medication

When it comes to the use of medication for mental illness-es, there are good reasons to try and use as little as possible for as short a time as possible. That said, psychiatrists have identified certain situations where they recommend the use of drugs over a longer period to try and prevent the recurrence of problems.

It is also sensible to view medication not as some kind of "silver bullet" but as one component of a wider treatment strategy. Healthy lifestyle choices in terms of diet, exercise and sleep are always wise. More specific interventions such as one of the talking therapies described in the next chapter may also be appropriate. Rather than seeing medication and talking therapies in terms of either/or, we should see them as both/and.

Where medication *is* used, we should see it, not as if it were somehow separate from faithful discipleship, but through the eyes of faith. Whenever science advances and effective medical treatments are developed, it can be seen as an outworking of gifts and resources that God has made available to us. Stewarding those gifts and making wise use of scientific advances is something we should seek to do and where they prove to be a blessing then we can give thanks to God for this gift of common grace. This will help ensure that our hope is not found, finally, in the pills we take but in the Lord who graciously provides all sorts of different people and resources to help us.

It is important to emphasise that any decision to take this kind of medication, or to stop taking it, or to change doses *absolutely must* involve medical supervision. These are complicated drugs with a wide range of effects and side effects. Those taking this kind of medication should seek and follow medical advice at all times.

A concluding illustration

Following an ankle injury, people often need to use crutches to support themselves. Usually such support is only needed for a time while healing of the ankle takes place. After that the support can, and should, be withdrawn. Indeed, continuing use of the crutches longer than is necessary may produce new problems in the ankle by preventing it from functioning normally. But some ankle injuries can be so bad that long-term support for the ankle is the only solution. Even in those cases, however, there will also be other things that can and must be done to support and care for the injured ankle alongside that ongoing physical support—physiotherapy and regular exercise, for example.[4]

This can be a helpful way to view the use of psychiatric drugs. They are the temporary support that can help manage the condition while other things are done to help improve things. But sometimes, the illness requires much longer-term use of drugs. In these ways medication can play a vital part in treatment.

---

4 This illustration is adapted from Mike Emlet's excellent little book *Descriptions and Prescriptions* (New Growth Press, 2017).

Questions for reflection

1. Have you ever taken a psychoactive drug (e.g. a tranquilliser)? How did you feel about it beforehand? How did it make you feel while you were taking it?

2. What stories have you heard about drugs being helpful, or profoundly unhelpful, for those struggling with mental illness? Do you think this has made you overly suspicious of drugs and their value in helping?

3. What would you say to someone who suggests that Christians should never take psychiatric drugs?

CHAPTER 5

TALKING THERAPIES

When we struggle with our mental health, many of us choose to talk about it. Usually that begins with family and friends. Faced with crushing anxiety and fear, weighed down by a gloom that never seems to shift, or battling with damaging habits we seem unable to resist, the very strangeness of those experiences will often drive us to speak with others. We want help to make sense of things we cannot compute. Talking it through seems an obvious first step. After all, as the saying goes, "A problem shared is a problem halved".

Only it's not always like that.

Sometimes the very strangeness of our experiences will silence us. How can we possibly find the words to express something so incomprehensible? What will people think of us? And naming things out loud gives them a reality that we are desperately trying to deny. We don't want this to be happening to us, and perhaps, by ignoring it, it might just go away. Then no one would ever know about the crazy thoughts we've been having. Sometimes opening up to talk can be very hard indeed.

This chapter explores some of the many different "talking therapies" that are available. Those facing struggles with their mental health will often be offered such help, so it is important to understand them. But first we should recognise how professional counselling and therapy sits alongside the many more informal ways by which talking can help.

Different kinds of talk

People will, generally, seek help for their mental-health difficulties from friends and family long before they approach a professional. And we should not underestimate the value of homespun wisdom coming from thoughtful life experience. Commonsense solutions shouldn't be dismissed lightly. Many difficulties have been nipped in the bud that way.

Indeed, for all their apparent complexities, all talking therapies have a few basic elements. First, someone listens and understands our experience. Then some kind of reorientation is provided that suggests a new way forward. Friends can do that, and so can pastors. There is enormous value in simply offering to talk something through, and we mustn't lose that.

A little orientation

Terms and titles used in this area can be confusing. The following list may help us navigate the complexities of this area.

Psychology is the study of the human mind and of its impact on human behaviour.

A **psychologist** will have trained in this field and a clinical psychologist has specialised in the mental-health aspects of psychology.

Psychiatry is the branch of medicine that deals with mental illness. A psychiatrist is a doctor who has completed a normal medical training (just like a surgeon or a paediatrician) but has then specialised in the care of people with mental illness.

Mental-health services generally organise themselves in **multi-disciplinary teams** made up of people from a range of professional backgrounds. Typically, they might include the following:

- Psychiatrists
- Psychologists
- Social workers

- Community psychiatric (or mental health) nurses
- Occupational therapists

And any of these people might provide talking therapy.

Psychotherapy is an umbrella term describing a whole range of talking therapies. The word comes from the Greek *psuche*, meaning "soul", and *therapeuo*, meaning to "treat" or "heal". Psychotherapy is, literally speaking, healing of (or by) the soul. It is used to describe a wide range of psychological treatments that rely on talking.

Counselling is, literally, the giving of counsel. Counsellors work in a range of areas—for example, career counselling, sports counselling and marriage counselling. Those who provide talking help may be identified by the counselling they do or the training they have received; for example:

- Psychodynamic psychotherapy
- Family therapy
- Cognitive behaviour therapy (CBT)
- Non-directive counselling

Some common ground and some differences

All counsellors and therapists seek to listen and to understand. Using good listening skills, they help people describe their experiences and the difficulties they are facing. Often there is an educational element to counselling—helping people understand what it is they are experiencing. Some counselling involves advice and guidance, but some definitely doesn't.

Non-directive counselling avoids giving advice or direction. Instead, through being provided with a space to think and explore, people are encouraged to arrive at their own decisions and solutions.

Experiential therapy/counselling describes approaches which rely on more tangible bodily or emotional experiences. Some see these as "bottom-up" rather than "top-down" therapies because of the way they involve some kind of physical experience rather than solely relying on thinking and talking alone. Play therapy and EMDR (eye-movement desensitisation and reprocessing) are two examples.

In individual psychotherapy someone sees a counsellor or therapist on their own, while in couple counselling two people in a relationship meet with a counsellor together.

In group therapy a collection of unconnected people are brought together for a series of meetings facilitated by a group therapist.

Qualifications and accreditation for psychotherapy practitioners vary widely. In some places (but not currently in the UK) "counsellor" is a protected term which can only be used by certain registered people. Accrediting bodies exist which may provide some kind of registration as well as overseeing training and practice. It makes sense, therefore, to exercise a degree of caution and to seek recommendations from others before seeking out help for our mental health.

Common counselling approaches

People generally seek counselling because something "hurts". And their ambition, generally, is that the hurt might go away. Not unreasonably, people often just want to know which counselling will take the hurt away fastest and furthest. Yet, as we will see, the various counselling approaches each hold a different perspective on people and their problems. They have beliefs about what goes wrong with people and why. They also have beliefs about what makes people better and, indeed, what that "better" state looks like. Some, or even all, of these beliefs may be fundamentally at odds with biblical thinking—all of which can make seeking out talking therapy a very complicated business. In the brief descriptions below, we'll imagine how each approach might seek to help **Sheila**, a woman in her 40s with depression and anxiety.

Psychodynamic therapy

Sigmund Freud's thinking is often trivialised or even ridiculed today. Yet he has exerted a profound influence on Western thought. Many ideas which are commonplace today found their origin with him. It was Freud who introduced us to concepts like repression, regression and projection, and it was Freud who first described the unconscious mind and who claimed that it revealed itself in dreams and errors of speech (Freudian slips).

Many psychotherapies used today are derived, to some degree, from Freud's ideas. So, while we cannot hope to adequately capture his thinking in a few short sentences, here is a brief summary. Freud believed that all of us need to develop emotional maturity. That maturity is marked by an ability to cope with the challenging circumstances of life as well as the challenging internal emotional experiences common to all of us. Freud believed that children need a secure caring relationship with their parents (or other primary carers) in order to manage the powerful (and rather dark) primitive emotions they experience. With such security, they develop healthy ways of managing those emotions—they become emotionally mature. Where children are denied a secure and stable upbringing, they develop much less adaptive methods of managing those emotions. He believed that in later life this failure to develop emotional maturity was revealed through disturbances of mood and in various relational difficulties.

In psychodynamic therapy, clients revisit these difficulties in the context of a secure and stable therapeutic relationship. This allows them to develop better, more mature ways of coping with emotions, replacing the immature ones which are creating difficulties for them. Unconscious fears and desires are brought into consciousness, and, instead of feeling controlled by forces of which they are unaware, a person grows in self knowledge and is able to make wiser and more mature decisions for their lives.

Psychodynamic therapy lasts longer than many other therapies and is usually more demanding emotionally. In Sheila's case, we might imagine her revisiting a sense of abandonment that she felt when her mother had a long stay in hospital and she went to stay with a strict and emotionally distant aunt. In the therapy, what initially seems to be anger towards her aunt gradually gives way to reveal Sheila's fear that her mother never really loved her and had sent her away not because she was in hospital but because she regretted ever having given birth to Sheila. This "psychodynamic" only reveals itself when the therapist misses some sessions through ill health. This absence precipitates a profound sense of "abandonment" in Sheila and is accompanied by a strong emotional reaction towards her therapist. This "transference" response—an emotional reaction to the therapist that echoes feelings properly belonging elsewhere—is then explored in the therapy.

Behaviour therapy

Behaviourism describes human activity in terms of stimulus and response: a stimulus, A, produces a response, B. If one set of learned responses are creating difficulties, the solution is to learn some new ones.

For example, a person with a phobia (an exaggerated fear response) of spiders might learn to react less fearfully to our eight-legged friends. The mechanism, which is called "exposure and response prevention", involves exposing someone to a feared object and allowing their anxiety to reduce to a more normal level. In this way they learn an appropriate, rather than an exaggerated, fear response. This therapy isn't really interested in what a person is thinking. All that matters is the way they respond physiologically and behaviourally. This is in contrast with cognitive behaviour therapy (CBT).

It would be unusual for behaviour therapy to be used as a main component in the care of someone like Sheila, who is experiencing depression. That said, depression can sometimes be associated with obsessive-compulsive features. If Sheila had developed obsessional behaviours because of a fear of contamination by germs, for example, then a programme of "exposure and response prevention" could possibly be used. But treatment aimed more specifically at helping with her depression would take priority.

Cognitive behaviour therapy

The Stoic writer, Epictetus, captures the essence of CBT in his observation that "people are disturbed not by things, but by the view which they take of them". For example, suppose a friend cancels their plans to come and see you for a weekend. That, in itself, isn't disturbing. It only becomes troubling if you take the view that they cancelled because they don't like you.

In this construction, because thoughts drive emotions it follows that if we can only take control of our thoughts then we can also take control of our emotions. "Negative automatic thoughts" (sometimes called "pop-up thoughts") leap into our minds and create unwanted emotional responses. For example: "If I don't get an A in this paper, I'm a failure"; "It's obvious they don't like me—they haven't phoned"; "I feel so useless at driving—I'll never pass my test".

CBT challenges this "faulty thinking" by arguing for a contrary view. Undermining these thoughts helps boost self-esteem and stops the negative emotions from being experienced. In CBT people learn techniques to challenge their faulty thinking and so keep negative emotions at bay.

Initially used mostly for depression and anxiety, CBT has since been applied to a very wide range of situations.

Sheila might perhaps be helped to notice ways in which she responds to feedback at work. Any encouragement is dismissed because "they're just saying that to be nice to me"; whereas even the slightest criticism prompts the thought that "no one believes I am up to this job and I'll never learn how to do it properly". In counselling, this thinking is challenged on the basis that Sheila has had several promotions and was specifically chosen for one particular project at a time when others in the company were being made redundant.

Person-centred (or non-directive) counselling

This approach has its origins in humanistic psychology which found the prevalent view of human nature in psychodynamic theory too dark and negative. They wanted to be much more positive about people and their potential for growth. In this approach to counselling, then, people are understood to have an innate drive toward growth so that, provided nothing hinders us, we will develop in a healthy and fulfilling way. People are designed to flourish, and only external factors stop us from doing so.

Through providing a positive, accepting and empathic relationship, person-centred counselling gives a context in which people flourish. They can get in touch with their true selves and realise their potential, becoming the best version of themselves that they can be. People don't need guidance or direction to achieve this (hence "non-directive" counselling)—they just require an affirming environment.

Sheila finds her counselling experience hugely encouraging. She feels that her therapist completely understands her, and she feels affirmed by them. She appreciates someone noticing her strengths and helping her to identify them. When she does express negative feelings, her counsellor listens and empathises, and this gradually helps her to understand why these thoughts have been so troubling to her. She finds herself able to accept her own strengths and weaknesses, and no longer blames herself for failings in the way she did previously. Overall, as the therapy progresses she notices a steady growth in her sense of confidence and self-worth.

Family and couple therapy

Many counselling approaches offer help to families and couples. Problems are explored through a consideration of wider relational networks. Because relationship systems are interconnected wholes, one part can't change unless the entire system changes. Problems are explored in relation to the whole system. So a child who is refusing to go to school may only be doing so because they are frightened by the conflict in their parent's marriage, and they imagine that staying at home may perhaps keep their parents together. Meanwhile, the parental conflict could itself be related to a demanding elderly parent who exerts a powerful influence over the wider family. Bringing effective change may require several different interventions simultaneously.

In a similar way, couple counselling doesn't so much explore the internal dynamics of each individual but the dynamic that exists in the relationship itself.

Perhaps Sheila attends counselling with her husband, and together they explore the disappointment they have both felt at being unable to have children. They come to realise that each of them feels profound guilt and sadness, but neither has felt able to tell the other because they have each been trying to look after the other and cope privately with their feelings of guilt. Couple counselling provides an opportunity to explore this disappointment in a context where they can listen to the other while someone else owns the responsibility to respond to the other's feelings.

Other approaches

Group therapy allows relational patterns to be recreated within the context of a group. Experiencing those relational tendencies and having them pointed out by others can be a powerful way to gain insight and change.

Integrative or eclectic counselling describes approaches

that make use of a variety of counselling approaches. Integrative counsellors combine elements from two or more approaches. Eclectic counsellors choose from a range of approaches, choosing the one they think would be most appropriate for each individual.

Reflections from a Christian worldview

Much could be said from a Christian perspective about the relative strengths and weaknesses of the various therapies described above. Space limits us to four general observations.

1. Common grace

Common grace is the term theologians use to describe how God shows kindness to everyone through the way the world works. So, although governments, systems and psychotherapists may not believe in God, nonetheless, what they do can be part of the way in which God shows his goodness to individuals. The doctrine of common grace teaches us to recognise that all good things come from the hand of our loving heavenly Father, even when those who deliver them do not themselves acknowledge God.

So we need not deny that there is much that is valuable and insightful in each of these approaches to therapy. We are affected by our past. Patterns in relationships do repeat, and one generation can pass failings to the next. Jacob deceived his father Jacob by pretending to be his brother Esau (Genesis 27). Later Jacob was himself deceived, first by Laban (Genesis 29) and then by his own sons when they told him that Joseph was dead (Genesis 37).

The Bible knows our tendency to be creatures of habit and how our thinking shapes us. These therapeutic approaches are noticing real aspects of the ways that human beings function. However, recognising that something contains truth doesn't mean it is comprehensively true.

2. Worldviews get imported

It is inevitable that the psychological assumptions under-pinning these therapeutic approaches will emerge at some point. For example, CBT brings with it a conviction about us needing adequate levels of self-esteem to flourish. But self-esteem isn't a biblical concept. The Bible is concerned with the way we do (or don't) esteem God and, of course, with God's estimate of us.

Similarly, the "realise your potential" theme that exists in person-centred counselling is a dominant theme in con-temporary culture. Yet the Bible teaches that while we are indeed fearfully and wonderfully made (Psalm 139:14), we are also ensnared by sin (Psalm 19:12; 51:3-5), and any en-couragement to fulfil myself can quickly become the basis for indulging my sinful desires and making life "all about me"—a profoundly un-Christian approach to life.

3. Experience matters

Identifying each expression of common grace in these ther-apies and carefully weaving them together with scriptural wisdom sounds like a perfect ideal, but the skills needed to do that aren't widely available, which means that those facing troubling mental-health difficulties can't usually afford to be fussy. Help is needed, and, sadly, there is often precious little professional help available—mental-health services are often underfunded and overstretched.

So it is right and proper to make use of mental-health services where necessary. These secular therapies can offer vital help for people in distress. What may be wise, however, is that those receiving such therapy find a godly Christian friend to help them reflect on the help they are getting. This may help them discover connections with Christ and the gospel as their therapy progresses. If we can relate the help we are getting to Scripture and to our relationship with the

Lord, the outcomes will usually be richer and more powerful as a result.

4. Biblical counselling

Ideally, we would weave all these elements richly together. Our churches would have the kind of helpers who know people, know their problems and are skilled and experienced in providing help. We would have built these things on the riches of Christ, who is our wisdom (1 Corinthians 1:24), and on his living and active word, which judges the thoughts and attitudes of our hearts (Hebrews 4:12). That, in one sense, is the ambition of biblical counselling: to aspire to just such wisdom and to deliver just such help.

But it takes time to grow in wisdom. And because the church has, for many years, been hesitant in its care of people who struggle with their mental health, we are starting from a place of relative poverty. But if we can redeem the wisdom found in psychology and learn to apply the grace of the gospel and the power of Scripture to one another's lives, we will have a talking therapy that surpasses all other talking therapies. We will profit from the ultimate psychotherapy— God's own gospel plan for the healing of our souls.

It is to this that we now turn.

Questions for reflection

1. Look back over the therapies described in this chapter. Which of these approaches, in essence, can come out in everyday conversations?
2. How do you feel about secular therapy and therapists? Are you basically suspicious or affirming?
3. What help do you think you need to "connect the dots" between therapy and theology?

SECTION 2

WHAT CAN
WE DO?

SECTION 2

INTRODUCTION

It's useful to understand mental health better, but understanding, in and of itself, is not enough. We still need to wrestle with the question: what, as a church, can we do to help those who are suffering? Or maybe, even, what should we do to help those in our congregations who are finding life hard? There are two important things to say up front:

1. **Doing *nothing* is not an option.** From the fall, believers have always struggled with their mental health—we will continue to do so until Jesus returns. There is no way of having a church that is free from suffering. It is the context in which all of us (to a greater or lesser extent) come to Christ and grow in him. And the Bible is clear that a normal congregation will contain significant numbers of people whose backgrounds are deeply broken (see 1 Corinthians 6). And those who are particularly burdened and weak are to be honoured, not pushed aside (1 Corinthians 12:22-23).

2. **Doing *everything* isn't an option either.** There are physiological complexities in some struggles, and churches are not places of pharmacological expertise. There is a right sense in which we are called to let the medical experts do what they do best, while we, as faithful followers of Christ, do what we do best—pointing people to the author and perfecter of faith. As Christians, we do not need to be suspicious of medicine,

nor do we need to imitate medicine and remould our churches into therapeutic communities, but we *can* celebrate all the wonderful ways in which medicine can alleviate suffering in the here and now.

Within those two extremes, however, there is a wide range of options. Some churches—as part of their discipleship or evangelism programmes—may specifically seek to reach out to those who are finding life particularly hard. Some churches will set up outreach programmes for those who are addicted; others will establish services that are uniquely welcoming to those whose mental-health struggles are profound. Other churches will simply seek to love those who are struggling but persevering.

Wherever we sit in that range of options, there is one thing of which we need to be convinced: God has a huge amount to say to those of us who are struggling with our mental health. Often we can forget that in our congregations. Sometimes we can focus on the past and future aspects of the gospel to the exclusion of all else. We remember that Jesus' death and resurrection has washed away our sin—we rejoice in the fact that his conquering of death opens the way to eternal life. But there is so much more. Scripture is overflowing with words of beauty and hope that enable all of us—whether we are struggling a little or a lot—to live a life worthy of our calling right now. The Bible has so much that can help us: comfort for past hurts, challenges for persistent sins, calls for better living, and coaching for complex circumstances. But, most importantly, it helps us engage with our Father, with our Saviour and with the Spirit who is living and active in all who believe in Jesus.

Our faith matters when we are struggling. And God's words are both tender and transformative to anyone who follows him. That doesn't mean that a sermon or a Bible study is going to take away someone's pain. Nor does it mean that if we get our teaching right then pastoral situations will naturally resolve. But it does mean that there is a huge amount we can all do to help those in pain—confident in God's generous provision of gospel hope, Scripture, prayer, people and his own indwelling Spirit.

In this second section of the book, we are going to focus on what is achievable for most churches, which is...

- helping people feel welcomed by raising awareness of common struggles.
- helping people feel loved by relating in Christ-like ways.
- helping struggling people to remember their true identity.
- helping people be refined to be more like Jesus, whatever their struggles.
- helping people persevere by means of the provision of resources from the wider church.

Will doing those things result in healing? *Not necessarily.* That is never promised this side of the new heavens and the new earth. But it will bring the hope and vital help we need to persevere through the difficulties.

CHAPTER 6

THE CALL TO RAISE AWARENESS

Struggles with mental health are a common human experience. They're a common Christian experience too. In any given church there will be a significant number of people who are suffering now or who have a history of finding life hard. Yet many people will attest to the fact that—within their congregation—they often feel alone or different, and certainly ill-equipped to connect the riches of Scripture to the realities of their daily life.

Any good pastoral response will involve a multifaceted approach, but the best and simplest place to begin is to *raise awareness*: to help people know that what they are experiencing is within the bounds of normal human experience, that they are not alone, and that there is hope and help both in the Lord and through his people.

Imagine **Tricia**—a middle-aged woman who's just been diagnosed with depression and prescribed antidepressants. She's still reeling from childhood abuse that has never been addressed. She's struggling with marriage tensions that are also not known about, and which she only superficially understands herself. As she walks into church as usual on Sunday morning, Tricia is carrying a world of hurt: feeling confused about how life has got this bad and worried about the future. But what is she walking into? A community where mental-health struggles are discussed with ease—both from the front and in quiet conversations? Or a community where no one says a word on these matters—or, at least, where very little is said and everyone feels a little awkward when the topic comes up?

Tricia's experience of her struggles, and her ability to turn to the Lord alongside her brothers and sisters in Christ, will be hugely impacted by her church context. In a church where conversations flow with appropriate ease, Tricia is likely to feel welcome, safe, accepted and hopeful. In a church where silence reigns when it comes to these areas, she is likely to feel ashamed, different, awkward and detached.

Here are four ways in which we can help Tricia—and, indeed, the whole congregation—to be more aware.

1. Sermons and Bible studies

Every preacher wants their sermons to make a difference—or, more precisely, for God to make a difference as his word is spoken into his children's lives in the power of his Spirit. It really is quite pointless to prepare a talk that merely informs people of something interesting about God's character or one that recounts a Bible story in a way that encourages people to respond merely by thinking, "Well, I never knew that!" Preaching isn't about the mere communication of information, nor is it even just about the explanation of Scripture (though those things play a part); it is one of the means of grace—one of the ways God changes his children to be more like him.

In a similar way, our Bible studies shouldn't be just "studies". Our midweek groups, our one-to-one meetings and our personal devotions aren't there to fill our minds with fascinating facts; they're there to fuel our souls: to encourage and excite us about the privilege that it is to live for Christ in this fallen yet hope-filled world.

In order to achieve these aims, preaching, teaching and Bible study need to help people connect the riches of Scripture to the realities of this life. And that means they need to be conducted in contexts where people can speak openly about just how hard some of those realities are.

An expository sermon or a Bible study on a single passage is rarely going to provide an opportunity for a talk on depression or anxiety. There is a place for topical talks, but an expository sermon isn't it. But it can be a place where people are regularly and repeatedly reassured that mental-health struggles are real, and that the passage under consideration has beautiful things to say to someone who hurts.

There are some obvious passages which speak specifically about mental health. Matthew 6:25-34, with its reminder that our heavenly Father knows what we need (v 32), is a glorious example—showing us that we are living our lives in the sight of a God who is aware of our struggles and who both cares and provides for us in the midst of them. It's also a passage that reminds us that God knows that we get anxious and fearful. The very fact that passages like this are in God's word demonstrates that anxiety is a common human experience. It doesn't tell us *everything* there is to know about anxiety—if we give people the impression that Matthew 6 is in some way a full antidote to anxiety, it will likely lead to more anxiety, if not despair. But the precious words of Jesus in this passage do provide a legitimate opportunity to raise the subject of anxiety, acknowledge that it's likely to be present in a wide range of people in the congregation, and allow the preacher or leader to give a few pointers to help sufferers.

There are other passages where Bible characters struggle with aspects of their mental health. Elijah's famous slump under the broom tree, where he prayed he might die (1 Kings 19:3-4), gives us a taster of the kind of despair that many with mental-health struggles experience. Heman the Ezrahite gives us a richer and more textured account of the experience of despair in Psalm 88 as he gives words to what many feel: that "[God has] put me in the lowest pit, in the darkest depths" (v 6). So many with depression can echo his sighs. Again, these passages aren't the place to explain depression or suicidal tendencies—they don't give a comprehensive account of someone's mental health—but they give us a glimpse of these realities and provide wonderful opportunities to say with confidence that it's normal for believers to despair sometimes and that God welcomes our cries when we do.

But it's not just the obvious passages that are useful for raising awareness in the local church. As we work our way through the Gospels in sermons or small groups, there is passage after passage drawing attention to God's character and mission. In those books we see Jesus' sovereignty, his tenderness, his call to community and his love. These are all aspects of God's work and ways that have beautiful things to say to people struggling with their mental health, if their attention is drawn to it.

Let's return to Tricia for a moment. No sermon is going to take away the horrors of past abuse. No Bible study is going to make her depression or marriage tensions all better. But if, over a period of weeks, she hears from a variety of passages and people that struggle is normal—indeed, to be expected in a fallen world—that God hears her cries, that God is providing for her as she limps, and that there is hope, then those little moments of awareness-raising can, cumulatively, make a difference.

And they won't just make a difference to her; they will make a difference to those who aren't struggling too. They will help her friends understand her circumstances and view them more compassionately, more biblically. They will give the wider church a vocabulary for encouraging her to persevere in the light of God's work. They will prepare people's hearts for the possibility that they might find themselves struggling in the future (and they don't need to be surprised if they do). And they will begin to develop a culture in the local church where it is ok, even good, to talk about mental-health struggles and talk about them in the light of God's word.

We're not suggesting that absolutely every sermon and Bible study should be used to raise awareness of mental-health issues. There are other challenges, such as debt or persecution, that we might want to raise awareness of too. And there are certainly some passages that speak into emotional and psychological struggles more appropriately than others—we don't want to start twisting Scripture to fit a mental-health agenda. But when there are people in the congregation hurting, and there is an abundance of compassion and strength in Scripture that can make a world of difference to their lives, why wouldn't we want to join the dots wherever we can?

2. Dedicated evenings

Sermons and Bible studies are likely to be weekly events in many church programmes—they are the mainstay of our corporate spiritual nutrition—but there's always room for something a little different. And that's where a more topical approach can be brought to bear.

One of the joys of a church calendar is the opportunity to throw in occasional evenings (or mornings) on specific mental-health topics. Anxiety, depression, self-harm, eating disorders, addictions, grief, anger and despair are all the kinds of issues that many in the congregation want to understand biblically—either for themselves or for others about whom they care.

Some churches will have a congregation member who can facilitate events like this with ease. Some will want to engage a specialist from a parachurch organisation to speak well into the situation.[5] Most churches, however, won't have specialists in each of those areas, and that's ok—most congregation members don't want to be trained counsellors or therapists. But most churches will have people who know enough, have experienced enough and/or have read enough to be able to share something that is of use. Maybe there's a doctor or therapist in your congregation who could give a 10-minute introduction to what a specific mental-health diagnosis actually means. Maybe there's a pastor in the church who could give a 10-minute overview of some of the things the Bible says. Maybe there's someone in the congregation who has experienced the struggle and is willing to share a little of what it feels like day by day. Maybe there's someone who has encouraged and prayed with someone who is finding life hard and can share some tips on what has (and hasn't) worked well. Maybe there's someone who can facilitate a discussion on the ways in which the church can help those who are finding life hard—or circulate a list of good resources with which people might like to engage. Together, a church can build an event that helps average Christians respond in wise and authentically Christ-like ways to those who are experiencing struggles.

Events such as these aren't just about information; they're about overcoming stigma and equipping communities to live life in such a way that everyone is loved, welcomed, and pointed to Christ, in every circumstance. They dispel myths, they remind Christians that everyone has a part to play in encouraging each other, and they make it easier for those whose mental health is a challenge to speak about it openly and to seek the help they need.

---

5 For organisations that could help with this, see the resources section on page 189.

They can also provide a helpful place where people can "own up" to their struggles, perhaps for the very first time, and find others who are struggling with the same things unknown to them. They can also bring together carers who are struggling with the sometimes relentless burden of living with a depressive partner or an anorexic child. A couple at one church we know, who struggled with depressive illness, very hesitantly offered to run a one-off Saturday morning coffee time so that sufferers and carers could simply share their experiences together and find mutual support. They were completely astonished, as were the ministry team, when almost half the congregations showed up.

3. Books and resources

When it comes to raising awareness, a church bookstall can have an extraordinary role to play. After a church meeting, when others are engaged in lively conversation, the bookstall is often a safe place to retreat to for those who are finding life hard. Coffee time after church can be one of the most difficult aspects of corporate worship—the pressure to have conversation in a crowded space can feel utterly overwhelming. There is "safety" in browsing. Engaging with a book means not having to engage with people. As a distraction technique, it's not a bad one—but it can be made even better if people can see there are books there that are speaking directly into their pain.

It's not just the reading of the books and other resources that is helpful (though clearly, reading is a good thing to do)—simply seeing a relevant book on the bookstall says, "This is a church where you and your struggles are welcome—we're going to do our best to accept, understand and walk alongside you with our eyes on Christ". And that is a wonderful message to get!

A physical bookstall will always be limited by size, and

mental-health topics are only ever going to be a component of the wider stock—but online bookstalls can be more extensive and there is plenty of scope for a wide range of books being held.

It's also useful to be aware of good books to recommend to people you get into conversation with. There's a list of helpful and accessible titles on page 189. It is important to read them yourself first to make sure that the book is the appropriate length, level and tone for the person you gift it to—no book is one size fits all. And it's always good to think about how that book can integrate into your overall support of someone: offer to read it with them, discuss it with them and/or follow up with them after they have had it for a while. The book will show that you care; continuing the conversation with them, using it as a stimulus, will show you are committed to them.

4. Testimonies

A final way to raise awareness of mental-health struggles is to encourage brothers and sisters to tell their stories. Whether that's in a formal way in a service, prayer meeting or evangelistic event—or informally over a cup of tea—it's helpful to share stories of how God is at work in the pain of mental suffering. There's more than one way to share a testimony: it can be in a spoken format—a talk, an interview, a quietly shared story—or written in a notice sheet, church magazine or personal note. It can even be turned into a song. Whatever the format, people can be encouraged by hearing that there is hope in the struggle, and how support and help was discovered and accessed.

One of the harder aspects of mental illness within the local congregation is that sneaking suspicion that God has been at work in the past (forgiving our sins) and he will be at work in the future (making us perfect in the new heavens and new earth) but that there's not a lot going on right now—that, somehow, God isn't particularly relevant or active in any mental-health struggles we are dealing with today. Testimonies show that God has not gone to sleep or ceased to care or found himself unable to provide; he's there, loving, ruling, equipping, leading and changing us in the ways he knows to be best.

There can sometimes be a pressure to focus on testimonies that go something like "I once was an addict, but now I'm free" or "I used to get anxious, but now I'm confident in Christ" and, of course, they can be glorious to hear, although this experience is not the norm and can raise false expectations for people. But, often, the most powerful stories are the ones that track "I used to be very anxious—I'm anxious still, but I'm learning to trust and discovering wonderful things about God and myself as I do". Testimonies that ooze God's character and activity, and very tangibly show how living life following him makes a difference to our struggles, can encourage perseverance and hope in astonishing ways.

Reasonable concerns?

Here, then, are four ways in which every church can raise awareness of mental-health struggles; four ways in which every church can send out a message that those who are struggling are loved and have hope in Christ; four ways that, we hope, are utterly achievable no matter what the size of the staff team or the congregation itself.

Sometimes church leaders worry that doing this might derail the church. Some are worried that raising awareness might open a floodgate of pastoral situations. Others are concerned that talking about topics like these might distract the church from its primary tasks of word ministry in teaching and evangelism. But when these narratives and ideas are integrated naturally into the life of the church—alongside evangelistic events, courses, events for young families and lunches for seniors—it can start churches on the path to being places where lives are honestly shared, burdens are mutually carried and gospel hope flows freely between congregation members in ways that build everyone up.

Just think about Tricia again. None of the above-mentioned awareness-raising will miraculously take her pain away, but if every week her ears hear that strugglers are welcome in her church, that God loves her, that there is hope, that help is out there, and that others have walked the same path and rediscovered some measure of joy, then coming to church will be something that lightens her heart, galvanises her resolve to persevere and equips her to live life, even under the burdens of mental ill-health. Raising awareness enables churches to be Jesus-centred purveyors of hope.

Questions for reflection

1. How do you think your church is currently doing in regard to mental-health awareness? What is on the bookstall? When was a mental-health condition last mentioned in a sermon or Bible study?

2. In your own church setting, how can you raise awareness of mental-health struggles? Who can help with this process of raising awareness?

3. Think of someone who is struggling. How might sharing your testimony or a giving them a book speak into their life right now?

CHAPTER 7

THE CALL TO RELATE

No one is designed to navigate this life alone. On the very first pages of the Bible, we see God's design for community. It wasn't good for Adam to be by himself, so God provided him with a companion: someone to "do life" with.

Throughout the Old Testament, we see God's people being led, together, by their king. The New Testament is equally clear that we, as Christians, are diverse yet united—one body, one building, under the lordship of Christ. To be a Christian is to be with others—sharing not just the gospel but our lives as well (1 Thessalonians 2:8).

Alone and lost

Many who struggle with mental illness, however, feel desperately alone. Some of them will have experienced painful trauma in the past that severed familial relationships. The betrayal of being beaten by the mother who was designed to nurture you, or raped by the father or uncle who was supposed to protect you, is utterly devastating. Such acts of evil leave people wounded by those who should have loved them, and their attitude towards relationships can become deeply distorted. Even when the experiences are not so extreme, many people with mental-health struggles have known the pain of relationship loss in the past, and that makes relating to people in the present hard.

It's not just family experiences that bring a sense of isolation; church experiences can bring that pain too. Sadly, there are those who have experienced toxic church cultures that coerced, controlled or even physically abused them. Such horrors are fertile soil for growing mental-health struggles and can make it desperately hard to trust any kind of church community in the present.

Then there are the thoughtless comments from fellow congregation members. Of course, in many churches there are wonderful examples of pastoral care, but it's not hard to think of that person who always says something deeply unwise. "You don't need a pastor—you need a psychiatrist." "Why don't you come back to church when you're feeling a little less tearful?" "It's taking you a long time for you to recover from this, isn't it?" Each comment throws salt onto already gaping relational wounds, and the isolation builds further still.

Feeling (and looking) different

The difficulties in self-care that illness can bring means that problems with getting out of bed, getting dressed, getting washed or eating a healthy diet can visually mark people out as different.

Medication—useful though it can be—sometimes has side effects that set people apart too. It can be hard for someone to focus and follow the nuances of a conversation, so their comments can feel out of place. It can be difficult for people to sit still, and their constant pacing can make normal conversation very stilted. Frequent requests for glasses of water to quench unrelenting thirst go against most expected social norms.

And then there are the internal voices too. Maybe not literal voices (though that can sometimes be the case) but the inner monologue that many struggling with their mind will know only too well: "No one wants you." "No one loves you." "No one will care if you stay away." "You're always going to be alone—isolation is your destiny." Such words are lies, but they shout loudly. They go against everything the Bible says and yet, in the depths of our despair, they are utterly convincing. And so people with mental illness often find it easier to withdraw or to relate in ways that ensure they minimise the potential for getting hurt again.

Such things build together to make mental illness a very lonely place. So it can be a transformative experience for those who are struggling to be surrounded by appropriate relationships of love where they can experience safety, trust, value and that mutual giving and receiving of help (in whatever ways they are able to).

Relating wisely

We need to understand this: *trust builds slowly.* Someone who is struggling with short-term mild depression will probably be able to give and receive love pretty naturally, but those on the more severe end of the spectrum may find it hard, if not impossible. There is absolutely no way that someone who has been deeply betrayed in the past is going to be able to trust a church leader or a congregation with ease. There is no sense in which someone whose crushing burdens have nudged them to spend the last 15 years fearing people or angrily pushing others away is suddenly going to turn into a confident, chilled friend in a few short months. Someone who truly sees themselves as a useless, worthless or pathetic individual is not going to be able to maintain healthy relationships of mutual trust—their skewed self-image will always impact how they view others.

One picture of change we get in the Bible is that of plants growing (for example, see Psalm 1:3 and Jeremiah 17:7-8). If my garden is anything to go by, anything beautiful takes many years and a lot of nurture to grow. The only things that pop up quickly are weeds. This image shows that the process of helping those struggling with their mental health to build strong relationships can be a long one. So it needs to be one that is shared.

There is a line to be walked here. Those who are struggling will often prefer to build up a relationship with just one person. That's completely understandable. If they have been significantly hurt in the past, then it might feel overwhelmingly hard to try trusting a range of people simultaneously. In fact, it might not just feel hard; it might feel deeply threatening. And, as churches, we will want to be alert to this and compassionate in it. People who are burdened don't need extra burdens.

However, those who are helping rarely feel able to maintain a one-to-one relationship with someone whose mental-health struggles are profound (and, sometimes, there may be safeguarding concerns which mean that meeting in a one-to-one context simply isn't safe or wise). The time and energy needed to build and maintain those relationships can be huge, and if one person is doing that alone then it's likely that the person helping will burn out and the person hurting will experience yet another rejection as their friend has to back away.

Often the best way forward is to chat with the person who is struggling, assure them that the church wants to love them well, and discuss the ways in which different people might play different kinds of support roles. It might be that there's only one person with whom they want to share deeply, but there may be others with whom they're happy to go for a dog walk or take a trip to the supermarket.

Alternatively, the person struggling may be so desperate for a connection that they call multiple people every day. Again, this is completely understandable. Isolation is so very painful; wanting to feel loved isn't weird or manipulative. But here the danger is that one person's phone calls or visits take up everyone's time, leaving little capacity to support other people in the church in need. The people receiving the calls eventually get overwhelmed and push the struggling person away. Doing so tends to compound that person's pain and, in turn, the socially inappropriate ways in which they relate. It can become a downward spiral—one that needs to be stopped.

It might be that articulating what appropriate engagement looks like might help. (Not everyone is able to do that without help.) It might be that boundaries are useful—maybe articulating who's available on which days of the week will bring more hope and less rejection. Ensuring everyone has protected time will prevent exhaustion and will enable people to be loving, kind and attentive when they are in that support role. The precise details of how things will work will vary from situation to situation, but clarity is always key. And that clarity will be helped if we ensure we never hold out promises like "Call me any time—I'm always here for you" because those are promises that no one but God can ever keep. Sometimes boundaries can be set just between two individuals. But sometimes a more co-ordinated approach across sections of the church may be needed—but always with the aim of loving people well.

Relating to brothers and sisters

With those wisdom considerations in mind, however, it is a wonderful thing to love someone who is finding life hard. Sometimes that sense of privilege slips from our thinking—what dominates our mind is how hard it can feel. But the Bible is clear that we are called to see those who are struggling as indispensable members of the congregation, who are worthy of special honour (1 Corinthians 12:23). It's worth letting that sink in for a moment: that precious image-bearer who is so very burdened is a priority, and they are absolutely worth the time and energy that we pour into them. They may not be our only priority, of course, but they are a significant one, and that can galvanise us to set aside quality time to walk with them.

Remembering that this role is a privilege will protect us from seeing people as "projects": people we just need to touch base with because it's our job, or people we think we can "fix" quickly. It will protect us from resenting how they take time away from other things. It will spur us on to want to know them deeply rather than just seeing the diagnosis and nothing more. It will encourage us to be creative in the ways we spend time with them.

Discussing the kind of support they would value is an important first step. People with mental illness are still people—they have preferences and can make choices, and it's good for them to express those well. We may not be able to say yes to all their requests, but we will hopefully be able to say yes to at least a few.

Some are looking to untangle past hurts in a biblical framework; others want an opportunity to sit and pray; many will value the provision of eating meals together or opportunities to spend time in someone's home, just being part of the family. There will be those who value lifts to appointments, a hand doing the cleaning, encouragement to take some exercise or help reading God's word. And all that can fit naturally into our routines. For example, if you are batch cooking some curry for the freezer, why not invite someone to join you? They can help chop the veg, and they can go home with a few meals for the days ahead.

Or if you have a quiet time each day, why not pick up the phone one morning a week and share it with someone who finds it hard to read the Bible alone? The dog needs walking every day, so why not go with a friend who will struggle to walk unless they have a friend? Exercise is great for people who struggle with their mental health. If you're writing out Bible verses for yourself, why not send some to others too?

There are many ways in which we can serve and encourage others. Our service won't take away mental-health struggles, but it will mean that people come to battle their struggles alongside others rather than on their own, and it will build their experience of positive relationships that can begin to heal some of the experiences of the past. That can make a world of difference to their ability to keep going. It can bring us much joy too.

Though it doesn't need to be a one-way street: most people love to be able to give something back. They may not be able to serve regularly on a rota—they may not want to be burdened with an additional to-do list—but it's good for them to have opportunities to do what they can. Offering people the chance to pray, cook, clean, write cards of encouragement to others, cut out crafts for children's activities or whatever else their gifting and capacity allow them to do is a wonderful thing. It may bring them purpose and joy in ways that being served never will.

Relating to the Lord

The primary relationship in any Christian's life is their relationship with God. He's the author of all things, the sustainer and the provider—he's the one who loves best, leads best and provides real and lasting hope. And that holds true for believers wrestling with mental illness too.

Some of those struggling will have big questions about God. These are typical questions that haunt people, and you should have a sense of how you might answer them.

- Why is he allowing this suffering?
- Is he really good?
- Is there hope of healing in this life?
- Why won't he take the pain away?

Some will want to run to God, seeing heaven as such an

alluring place that they want to fast-track their arrival there through direct suicide attempts or living a reckless way of life. Still others will have a deep faith, clinging on to God with absolute surety in the hardest of times. A few will suffer delusions: a deep conviction that they are God or one of his messengers, with new insights that no one else can possibly hope to know. Everyone will be unique, and getting to know how the individual in front of us is experiencing faith is vitally important; otherwise we might make assumptions about their relationship with God that are far from true.

But for all those who are finding life hard, part of the church's role is to encourage them (and those seeking to help them) to turn to the Lord in the midst of pain. And that means encouraging everyone to relate to God in the whole spectrum of ways that the Bible sets out, including:

- **Praise**: We can ask the person what they would like to thank God for. Some people like to keep a journal of thanksgiving. Others like to write down one good thing every day on a piece of paper and stick it in a pot. At Sunday lunch, before tucking in, it can be a good discipline to go round the table and thank God for one thing that's been experienced that week. Maybe creating a playlist of favourite, faithful songs can fuel times of praise. Find something manageable that helps people lift their eyes and remember the generosity of God.

- **Lament**: Life is hard, and there are things—past and present—to weep over. Encourage people to read the Psalms or write their own laments and to pour out their hearts to God. It's ok to tell God that life feels awful. We don't need to pretend it's ok. Where possible, finding the words to say to him, "I'll trust you anyway" can be a great place to land.

- **Intercession for self:** We can encourage people to explore the richness of prayer. Some may find it hard to pray for themselves. Others will focus on prayers for healing. That isn't a wrong thing to pray for, but there's so much more: together, we can pray for perseverance, Christ-likeness, hope, faith and love, to name but a few.

- **Intercession for others:** Personal pain can feel overwhelming, but helping people pray for others is wonderful too. These might not be long and detailed prayers but perhaps just some post-it notes with prewritten prayers. Asking God to bless those persecuted for the faith, or the lady down the road now unable to leave the house, can be a wonderful way to serve others.

- **Bible-reading:** Listening to God's word together is a beautiful thing. Some people will be able to keep coming along to a Bible-study group or a one-to-one even during bleak days, but others will struggle to concentrate for the length of time that a formal group may require. Visiting someone, picking two or three verses of Scripture, reading them aloud and asking simply what those verses tell us about God and ourselves may be more than enough for someone who is finding life hard.

- **Corporate worship:** Sunday gatherings are important, but not everyone will be able to engage with them well. We can welcome people in for a few moments and let them leave. We can say it's ok to sit at the back and just listen—no need to stand. We can remind the rest of the congregation that if someone wants to pace at the back, then we love them in that—it's no big deal. Having an ethos of "It's great to have you here, however you can manage" will speak volumes to a wounded heart.

As we enact strategies like these, people will grow in their confidence to turn to the Lord, and that is always a good framework for enabling someone to persevere.

Questions for reflection

1. Think about the rhythm and routines of your daily life. What regular activities could you invite someone else to share with you as a way of encouraging them?

2. Are your boundaries with those who struggle a bit high or a bit low? How can you tweak them to a healthier place?

3. Think of someone who is struggling right now. How can you walk alongside them in a process of lament?

CHAPTER 8

THE CALL TO REMEMBER

I n mental illness, identity often gets skewed. We forget who we really are. Struggling believers can often see themselves in the light of what has happened to them ("I'm the abused one"), what's been spoken over them ("No one will ever love you"), or the diagnosis given to them ("I'm an addict"). Rather than seeing themselves as a precious, loved, child of God, their self-image is distorted into something ugly. Often, they can hate who they view themselves to be.

In a not dissimilar way, in mental illness God's identity can become distorted too. We forget who he really is. People may have a *taught theology* that is faithful—they can articulate what the Bible says—but their *functional theology* (the beliefs that drive their actual behaviour) might be much more moulded by their experiences than the word. That means it might well be much easier for them to see God as distant, uncaring, controlling or punishing than it is to see him as gracious and kind.

Any pastoral care of people struggling with their minds is likely to involve helping them to see God as he truly is— and to see themselves as God sees them too.

Remembering who God is

Every struggler will have a different story, but many will find it desperately difficult to believe that God really is as good as the Bible says.

Take **Jamie**, for example—a young man reeling from the

legacy of an abusive father and a daily battle with suicidal thoughts. Having been beaten regularly, ground down by being repeatedly told that his father wished he'd never been born and frequently left without adequate nutrition, his concept of "fatherhood" is now infused with nothing but fear and revulsion. Hearing that through Jesus he can come to know God as his heavenly Father may, initially at least, bring little comfort. Why would he want a father figure with even more power? To Jamie's ears, turning to a Father has little appeal.

Or consider **Marina**, an older woman who faces overwhelming anxiety every day. Life feels unrelenting to her. She is aware that many Christians get great comfort and strength from God's word, but when she reads of the call to pick up her cross and follow Christ—or is reminded of her responsibility to use her gifts in the service of the local church—it feels like one thing too many. God doesn't feel like a loving Saviour but more like a taskmaster constantly demanding things she cannot give.

Or what about **Neil**, a middle-aged man who has been hearing voices for years? He's frequently convinced that God is speaking to him, but the words he hears are rarely in concert with what has been written down. He may be aware that Christians believe the Bible to be authoritative, but the messages in his mind shout more loudly than any word on a page or voice from a pulpit. It's hard to believe that God isn't the controlling, coercive manipulator that Neil is "told about" in his head every day.

These distorted views of God are likely to have a devastating impact on these people's lives. Seeing God as threatening will make turning to the Lord in prayer feel impossible. Seeing God as a taskmaster will likely lead to withdrawal from him (and his people) or to a stoic attitude that believes serving just needs to be endured to placate the one who burdens those who follow him. Behaviours become motivated by fear or guilt. True faith, so full of freedom, becomes distorted and replaced by harsh religion.

Forgiven, secure and free

How important then to help people who are struggling with their emotions to see the greatness—and the goodness—of God. How wonderful to enable them to know that they are forgiven, secure and free.

When opening Scripture, it's often best to head first towards pictorial metaphors or narrative stories. Propositions—statements of truth—have to jostle for position with people's preconceptions. Reading "God is love" often elicits a simple response in the human mind—"He doesn't love me"—and people move on. While there may be an acknowledgement that the Bible is true, the truth doesn't land in people's minds, and so it doesn't stick. Stories and pictures speak in different ways: they seize the imagination, they tap into the affections of our heart, they provide concrete illustrations of what love looks like day by day and they embed themselves in the memory, providing fuel for reflection that lasts.

There are hundreds of stories in the Bible to tell. The horrors of Joseph's life not only provide an understanding that this life can be awful but also that God has good purposes that run far deeper than the pain. Ruth's journey from Moab to Israel shows us much of how to trust God with an unknown future and a family life that is in tatters. The wanderings of the Israelites in the desert illustrate clearly what it means for God to provide for his people one day at a time. The book of Lamentations—and many of the psalms—give words with which to respond to periods of devastation. Jesus' interaction with the women at the well in John 4 reminds us of the tender way in which God reaches out to those on the edge of society. The restoration of Peter after he let Jesus down helps us see how eagerly Jesus welcomes back those whose actions have been far from what we might hope.

There are multiple metaphors too. Dwelling on what it means for God to be a refuge when life is terrifying, or our King when life is confusing, or our Shepherd when life is exhausting, can be fertile ground for growth. Picking just one metaphor and digging deep into its meaning and relevance for several weeks in a row can help to really embed the goodness, safeness and generosity of God in someone's mind. There will be a few people for whom metaphors aren't appropriate—some in the midst of their struggles find it hard to grasp anything that isn't concrete—but many will value the richness of pictures that illuminate who God is.

It can be useful to open Scripture in very easy ways. An hour-long Bible study is unlikely to land well. Reflections on key verses, some faithful paraphrasing of longer narratives and occasional use of books that visually retell passages can all have their place. Limiting questions to ones that are easy to comprehend is wise. It can be helpful too to talk about all three Persons of the Trinity—someone who has been abused at home may find the concept of a Father hard to respond to, but the reality of a Saviour or a Helper will be much easier. In the initial stages of conversations, we meet people where they are at rather than dragging them to a place that feels too hard to endure. But little by little, the true nature of God can come into view—and people can begin to see that he is kind, welcoming, loving, safe, gracious, merciful and so much more.

Trauma and the Bible

Sadly, there are people whose mental-health struggles are rooted (at least in part) in Bible study that has been used abusively. There are people who have been subjected to ugly twisting of Scripture and have been manipulated into all kinds of pain on bogus biblical warrant. There are people who have been physically hit with God's word. There are people who have been told to cover up awful crimes or remain in deeply dangerous relationships on the basis of "forgiveness". There are others who have been made to memorise verses that speak of their depravity but ignore their value as image-bearers. Such things are a perversion of God's word and can leave people deeply traumatised.

When the Bible has been weaponised in this way, opening Scripture with someone may well not feel safe for them at all. It can be tempting to press on and think, "This person just needs a good experience of God's word", but the reality is we can cause far more harm than good by opening God's word with someone before they are ready. If you find yourself in this situation, the best course of action is to (a) pray quietly, (b) consult a trauma specialist and encourage the person to get the help they need to address the underlying trauma, and (c) ask the person how best the church can help. Some may want to chat about God's word (the emphasis here being on talking about it rather than being told what to believe); others will just want to experience loving community for now, and that's ok. When the Bible feels dangerous, giving people time (as much time as they need) to feel safe is important.

Laying the groundwork for change

It's worth saying that when someone is struggling, we might have to start our Bible studies in a different place from where we would start with someone who is well. An individual who is feeling positive and eager to learn will probably be willing to engage with any part of the Bible, but someone who is feeling broken may find the process of even opening the pages of a Bible hard.

A simple preparatory structure that might be useful is to explore each of these areas in turn:

- **How do they see God?** As distant, capricious, impotent, unloving, coercive, revelling in people's pain, a taskmaster, a benign Father Christmas, an uncompromising judge demanding justice or something else? It's worth taking time to get as rounded a picture as possible of what someone is thinking so you know where your starting point is.

- **How did this view of God develop?** Are they seeing God in the light of a significant person in their life? Are they focusing on just part of God's character—a part that fits with their pre-existing assumptions? Are they listening to voices or other, external sources of information?

- **How much evidence do they feel they have for this perspective?** There's a world of difference between someone who is feeling down and temporarily can't see the goodness of their heavenly Father and someone who has had 35 years of unrelenting pain from their earthly father and can't even begin to believe that fatherhood can be associated with love and safety. Sometimes people have good reason for being confused, and it's worth acknowledging the power of those reasons.

- **What would make it safe for them to consider changing their views?** Emotionally, there can be a huge cost in letting go of preconceived ideas of God—a cost that might seem far too high unless steps are taken to make things easier. After all, avoiding an earthly father may have been an essential strategy for surviving childhood; being asked to engage with any father (even a heavenly one) might feel like a life-threatening event. And reading God's word may well be encouraging in the end, but to the anxious mind there will still be a pain-barrier to overcome in terms of wrestling with the passages that feel hard. It might mean choosing a particularly safe place in which to read God's word (and that might not be a church) and being accompanied by a safe person (which, if you are an authority figure, might not be you).

- **What foundations need to be put in place before change can begin?** Even when a person feels it is safe to look at God's word, it may not be wise to dive into passages that address directly their misunderstanding of God. Sometimes there's preliminary work to do. Jamie may need to see passages that speak of God's hatred of abuse (in the minor prophets) before he can hear stories of a heavenly Father's love. Marina may value reading stories of biblical characters who felt overwhelmed (such as Elijah) to show that her experience is not unique and not a barrier to engaging with God's word well. Neil may benefit from some big-picture thinking on the consistency of God before he is ready to review the "new revelations" he holds so dear. Before building an extension on a house, lots of time is spent in levelling out the foundations—it's the same in pastoral care. We'll want to help people get their foundational understanding in place before the tough work of helping people change their perception of God begins.

- **Are there realistic expectations of change?** Some people have a good capacity to understand what the Bible says—others less so. And while we always want to acknowledge that God is able to do immeasurably more than we ask or imagine (Ephesians 3:20), it is far from definite that someone who is experiencing delusions long-term will be able to grasp what is true. They will be able to change a bit, as every human can, but they simply might not have the capacity to change a lot this side of the new creation. Aiming for a bite-sized change may be wise. Perhaps we could encourage Neil simply to get to the place where he comes to chat to an elder about any new revelations—acknowledging that he might not always be right.

With these things in place, people are far more likely to be able to hear words of truth. They will be far more receptive to the idea that their experiences—though deeply scarring—do not have to be defining when it comes to how they view God. The word can be heard more clearly and gradually believed. It won't happen overnight—growth is nearly always slow—but little by little, people can come to see that God is good.

Remembering who *we* are

Within evangelical circles we often have an uneasy relationship with self-image. Some buy into the culture of self-esteem and encourage everyone to think well of themselves. Others hold firmly to the total depravity of the human heart and confidently assert that, in and of ourselves, there is nothing loveable within. It can be hard to hold in tension the two biblical truths that humans are rebels but, in Christ, we are lavished with grace, loved, valued and clean.

Those struggling with their mental health often have a particularly low self-image. The words that have been spoken over them in the past, the way they are so often treated and the negative emotions going through their minds will frequently nudge them to think of themselves as useless, pathetic worms who can never be loved and never have purpose or hope.

However, many will also be familiar with pop psychology and its memes, which encourage people to be proud of who they are, to cut out anyone who doesn't accept them and to avoid any talk of sin or wrongdoing. The message that often rings loudest is that people are victims—unwell and only need of acceptance, never challenge.

Both poles are dangerous places to be. On the one hand, to live with a perception of oneself that is so low that it denies the wonder of being made in the image of God is to be condemned to a lifetime of self-loathing. For any individual to think of themselves so poorly that they forget they are a beautiful and precious child of the living God jars horribly with the psalmist's contention that they are "fearfully and wonderfully made" (Psalm 139:14). But, on the other hand, to have an expectation that all we should experience is affirmation will leave non-Christians isolated from salvation and Christians isolated from the means of progressive sanctification that the Bible holds out. As believers we want to hold out something better.

In pastoral care, our goal is to help people shift their eyes from the rose-tinted mirror of the world and from the bleak mirror of their experiences (past and present) and their interpretation of them, and instead to turn their eyes to the mirror of the word, where they can begin to glimpse how precious they are in the sight of God and yet how desperately in need of change we all are.

Ephesians 1 is a wonderful place to spend time in. It's one of the key passages in Scripture that helps us see ourselves as God says we are as followers of Jesus. There we discover we are chosen, called, lavished with grace, forgiven, adopted, indwelt by the Spirit, blessed and heading for an inheritance beyond compare. There we see our deep need of God (because we are not ok as we are) but also the deep generosity of God, whose work genuinely does transform us into someone new. We are loved. We are clean. We are secure, if we are in Christ.

There's too much in Ephesians 1 to grasp in one sitting. We'll need to help people go back time and again. Putting key words into an infographic, memorising the odd verse here or there, coming back to phrases repeatedly, or asking the question, "What difference does knowing you're chosen make today?" can all be helpful techniques. Backing up the teaching of Paul with Bible narratives can add depth too. The common thought that "Maybe God does forgive most people, but he hasn't forgiven me" can helpfully be addressed by looking at the horrors of David's life and his response in Psalm 51. The forgiveness that is lavished on him can help others realise that the same kind of grace can be lavished on them.

Change will inevitably be slow, but gradually people can come to see themselves as they truly are. Understanding truth about God and themselves won't erase mental illness, but it will provide a beacon of hope within it. Being ill before a vicious god is a terrible thing—being ill in the loving arms of a kind God is a very different experience. Struggling with illness while feeling like the world would be better off without you is horrifying. Struggling with illness knowing that it doesn't define you and that, even at your weakest, you're still passionately loved is a place of great comfort and hope.

Questions for reflection

1. Have you ever struggled with seeing God as fundamentally good, gracious and kind? What helped you see God more clearly?
2. How do you hold together the two truths that you are wonderfully made and loved, and yet fallen and sinful? How would you explain that to someone who struggles to understand it?
3. How flexible are your methods in opening Scripture? How could you grow in this area?
4. Think of someone who is suffering with their mental health. Where in Scripture might you go to help them remember just how good God is?

CHAPTER 9

THE CALL TO REFINE

Should we expect those with mental-health struggles to change? It's a controversial question. You might have heard people suggest that mental illness is just like physical illness and we shouldn't expect ill people to change any more than we would expect someone with a broken leg to walk. (That thinking conveniently forgets that, in some physical illnesses, lifestyle and mindset changes can be deeply significant in recovery.)

You may have heard others argue that change is an expected process for all Christians. God is at work in the world and all but the most extremely unwell have some capacity, so some change *must* be expected. Still others promise full and final healing in this life, confident that God is both willing and able and that therefore his miraculous touch will be seen. It can be troublesome to work out where the truth is to be found.

To expect no change can sound freeing. Often, church communities expect those with mental-health struggles to change far too quickly and far too completely. But if no change is expected, it allows people the space in which to struggle without pressure and removes unhelpful expectations that they should be "getting better". It also ensures that no one feels condemned for not being able to cope or not being able to think clearly enough. It acknowledges that genetics, wayward biochemistry and other bodily responses to hard things are physiological realities that can't be ignored. And it encourages congregations to continue to bear with those whose behaviour might seem confusing or hard rather than press them for what they are not able to give. *Case closed?*

Not really. Expecting no change can also sound hopeless. To suggest that God can offer nothing but a pair of loving arms in which to rest until the new creation makes God seem very small. To intimate that the process of change brought by the Spirit is out of reach to those with mental-health struggles is deeply unwise. God does not show partiality to his children—he does not withhold his Spirit from believers who are unwell. There must always be hope of some change.

But overpromising change does no good either. At worst, we promise now what God has only promised in the new creation (what theologians call "over-realised eschatology"), and that will only ever lead to disappointment and despair. It's far better to discuss with the person struggling what a baby step of change might look like. Far better to pursue something small, desirable and achievable than expect fast, unsustainable change.

Small steps

Meet **Li**, a young woman from China who has a diagnosis of bipolar. Some weeks she struggles to get out of bed; other weeks she barely sleeps as she hurtles from a cleaning spree to a mammoth online shop. She phones congregation members frequently—often at inappropriate times of the day or night—and talks incessantly and angrily about the church, politics and her latest conspiracy theory. She swings between being convinced that she's trash to being absolutely sure that she's the only one with insight. Sometimes she takes her medication; sometimes she doesn't. Life is desperately painful for her. It's not easy for those around her either.

What change would you want to see in Li? It might be tempting to say, "I want her to stop phoning, to start containing her emotions, to think clearly, to speak rationally and to take her medication regularly". On one level, I suspect Li would want that too. But that's not actually a realistic goal—not in the short to medium term, at least. Step One is much more likely to involve helping Li see that, in Christ, she is safe—loved—and so she can pour out her heart to God.

Refining safely

It's important not to underestimate the importance of safety. No one is going to change for the better in a context where they feel under threat. Impatience, intolerance, unrealistic expectations or simplistic solutions will inevitably result in someone feeling unloved and therefore deeply unwilling or unable to engage in any process of change.

People change when they know they're loved—when they know there's a real, meaningful relationship; when there is a realistic, mutually understood and agreed plan rather than an unwelcome, unilaterally imposed one.

That doesn't mean we should pour limitless time into someone—boundaries are essential in all relationships—but it will mean discussing those boundaries. People who struggle with their mental health have often experienced multiple people pushing them away; boundaries will feel like another rejection, unless articulated with care.

Refining wisely

Before attempting to go on a journey of change with someone, it's also important to think through what is safe to address in a church setting and what needs to be undertaken in a more formal setting or with professional help.

Trauma is a complex area. It would be deeply unwise for the average pastor or congregation member to encourage someone to relive a traumatic event to try to address flashbacks. Reliving trauma is in itself deeply traumatic and, if it is to be undertaken at all, it certainly needs to be done alongside someone with significant training and relevant experience.

Trauma that has been experienced in a church context is something that requires particular care. God's word is full of hope. It is beautiful and rich. But there are some who have experienced the horrors of the Bible being weaponised. There are those who have endured great abuse under the pretext of fulfilling some biblical command and others who have been silenced by the angry quoting of out-of-context verses. There are even those who have been physically beaten with Bibles when they failed to submit. There are precious brothers and sisters who love God but whose experiences lead them to self-harm or dissociate (cut themselves off from reality) every time Scripture is read because the wounds caused by wolves in the church are just too deep. The ugliness of such experiences is impossible to express. The very act of opening a Bible with someone who has been through such trauma can leave them reeling and broken. We can pray there will come a day when they can open Scripture with joy again—that is an aim—but time, compassion and much painstaking work is needed before that can happen. Most untrained people will find it impossible to help constructively.

Similarly, someone experiencing delusions or psychosis may well need some measure of medical stabilisation before anything else can be addressed.

As church leaders and church members we need to be simultaneously confident in our great God, who can bring real change, and acutely aware of our limitations. Just because God can bring great change doesn't mean he is going to use us at the centre of that change process. He may well opt to use someone far more skilled than us, and it is an act of wisdom and spiritual maturity to realise that our role may be on the periphery of a pastoral situation rather than at the centre.

Refining by normalising the abnormal

But there will always be something we can do. If God has placed a struggling person in our lives, then we have some responsibility to support them. Sometimes mental-health struggles can seem very confusing and beyond our comprehension, but there will always be points of contact with what we understand.

Depression is more than sadness, but if we have tasted sadness, we will know how important it is to see that God is the God who brings hope. Anxiety is more than fear, but if we have ever been scared, we will know how important it is to wrestle with what it means to live life under the protection of the God who is our Rock and Refuge. Addictions are more than indulging too much, but if we have ever found ourselves craving something that isn't good for us, we'll know how crucial it is to remember that God offers a life that is better than any substance can bring. By normalising the abnormal, we can get a tiny glimpse of what our friend is experiencing and begin to think about what pictures of God will help them persevere.

Refining imaginatively

Often people with mental-health struggles will feel hopeless. They may have been unwell for some time. They may have tried many things that haven't worked. They may have been criticised or condemned for not changing. Those things often lead people to believe that any change is impossible—that they are doomed to the same thoughts, emotions and behaviours that have been part of their life for years. Before embarking on a process of change, it's often essential to cast a vision for that change. It's important to dream some dreams of how life could be.

While some people can move away from their mental-health struggles fairly fully—many cannot. All of us will struggle with something for our whole lives, and mental health may be that struggle. So, while there are moments when we may want to cast a vision of complete freedom (e.g. in the case of addiction), most of the time we'll want to be more nuanced than that. We can dream of…

- **Complete healing in the long term.** The new heavens and the new earth are going to be wonderful—not a hint of mental illness will be found. We can remind people that this time is coming and it's going to be good. There may need to be some caution here: telling people in the pit of despair that heaven will be great can inadvertently encourage suicidal tendencies to build. There may be moments when we choose not to dwell on eternity for that reason. But even when someone has no suicidal thoughts or plans (what professionals sometimes call "suicidal ideation"), it can be wise to throw in reminders that perfection comes in God's good timing, not ours.
- **Thriving in the medium term.** Mental-health struggles will always be hard, but they do not have to be devastating. It is possible to have a decent quality of life with most struggles. We can help people dream of a life with good relationships, a right view of God and self, and a deep sense of purpose.
- **Persevering with hope in the short term.** Even today there will be something—someone—to hold on to. And that hope can make all the difference in the world.

We can be confident that it is possible for believers with mental-health struggles to gradually grow in the knowledge that God is good: we are his precious children, we are not alone, we can begin to see the light in dark places, we can learn to relate differently to others, the wounds of the past can begin to heal, there is justice, there is security and there is a reason to keep going.

Understanding the process of change

With these building blocks in place, people can be ready to engage in the process of change: a process which the Bible describes as being like changing our clothes.

Ephesians 4:22-24 reminds us that all disciples of Christ have a call:

> *You were taught, with regard to your former way of life, to put off your old self, which is being corrupted by its deceitful desires; to be made new in the attitude of your minds; and to put on the new self, created to be like God in true righteousness and holiness.*

That's not a passage to be used simplistically. We're not called to take off our mental-health struggles, think happy thoughts and go on our way in perfect health. It's not a passage to be applied thoughtlessly. There will be some things we can't take off and put on. With the best will in the world, we can't take off a physical ailment like a broken arm; we can't simply "take off" the fact we have been abused. But when used in relation to things that *can* be taken off and put on—and used to encourage change at a speed that allows people to grow gradually—there is much change that can be pursued.

Everyone who is struggling will have some wayward beliefs about God, his world and their part in it. For example, someone who is depressed may think, "God doesn't love me". That's an "old self" thought. It's not in line with a new life in Christ. We don't want to make people feel guilty for thinking it. There will be reasons why they believe it to be true—it's not just a whim. But we can gradually encourage strugglers to spot the untruth every time they think it, and rather than leaving it unchallenged, to start thinking, "I feel as if God doesn't love me, but the Bible says otherwise".

Over a period of time, we can encourage the people around us to progress in the process of "taking off" that thought a little more. We might encourage people to catch each incidence of "God doesn't love me" and turn it into a prayer: "I feel as if you don't love me, Lord, but I know you want me to believe you do. Please help me to want to turn from what I believe to what you say." In doing this, we've helped precious image-bearers to move from noting their thoughts to bringing their thoughts to God.

A little later, we might encourage people to progress to a prayer of confession: "Sorry, Lord—I keep thinking you don't love me. I know your word says you do. Thank you that you are going to help me stop buying in to the lies of my past and be confident in who you are and what you say." Here we're facilitating some gentle repentance and helping people articulate what's true, in an attitude of confidence in the Lord.

It's tempting to rush this process—to fast-pace it into a week. *It won't work.* It may well take months—maybe years. But little by little, with plenty of prayerful encouragement from us, the old self can begin to loosen.

Along the way, engaging with God's word helps our friend's mind be renewed. We can look at statements that say God loves them (John 3:16 or 1 John 3:16). We can look at stories that show God's love: to Peter (even though he messes up); to Elijah (even though he despairs) or to Ruth (even though she has nothing to offer). We can look at psalms that articulate God's immeasurable goodness and care. We can take them to the cross of Christ and help them see there just how overwhelmingly loved they are by the one who was willing to die and rise again for their salvation (1 Peter 1:18-19). Or we can simply talk about the evidence for God's love that we see in our own lives.

And we can pray for the person that we are walking alongside—simply but consistently—that they will grasp how wide, long, high and deep is the love of God (Ephesians 3:18). God is at work in us all.

And when the time is right, we can talk to people about the possibility of putting on their new self. To start by praying prayers like "Thank you, God, that you love me—even on the days I don't feel it". To grow in confidence in the Lord by writing their own simple prayers or psalms of praise. To develop a habit of gratitude (for example, thanking God for one thing every morning and every night) in order to regularly bring to mind God's love and to praise him for it. And to consider, step by step, what it means to live in the light of that love.

All humans change slowly. Those who are struggling may change particularly slowly—they're following their Saviour with a more pronounced limp than others. But there is hope. And once someone begins to change, there is no telling how exciting that change might become.

Questions for reflection

1. What has your experience of change and growth as a Christian been over the years? Is it continuing now, or are you "cruising"?
2. Are you more likely to push for quick change or pull back from encouraging any change? How do you need to change in this area?
3. Think of someone you know who is struggling at the moment. What one small thing can you encourage them to take off or put on this month?

CHAPTER 10

THE CALL TO PRACTICALLY RESOURCE

In New Testament times, widows were a vulnerable group. With no husband to take care of them—and no guarantee of a son who might do the same—the money needed for food could be hard to find. Taking care of those widows within the church had some challenges. At times, certain groups of widows were left out, and that caused real pain.

A system had to be put in place to ensure the fair distribution of resources (Acts 6). But even though it proved tricky at times, there seemed to be a shared assumption in the early church: *Christians provided for other Christians in need.* Doing so is simply an expression of the truth that those who belong to Christ belong to each other.

It wasn't just food that Christian believers shared with each other—money and other possessions were generously distributed besides. Christ-centred communities, where people share lives, naturally result in people meeting each other's practical needs (Acts 4:34-35). Indeed, the Bible says it would be utterly inconsistent to be Christians who claim to want the best for people but then don't act practically for the good of those around us (James 2:16).

For most of us today, shopping, washing, cooking, cleaning, gardening, walking the dog and paying the bills are tasks that simply get done. They might be a bit of an irritation, but it wouldn't occur to us to leave them undone. For people who are struggling, however, they can be a burden too far. Even those with relatively minor struggles with their mental health may skip meals; those whose struggles are profound may well find the simplest acts of daily living hard to grasp. And, as with the early Christians, it is our privilege to rally round wisely and well.

Resourcing those struggling

When someone is finding life hard, the best place to start is to ask them what help they would like. Even if they do not know the answer to that question, they will probably appreciate being asked. Having the humility to pose the question (rather than assuming we know) and the willingness to act on the answer is, in and of itself, an act of love.

Asking also prevents us from defaulting to convenient but unwanted acts of care. It's a depressing reality that many of the well-meant meals that are delivered to people's doors end up in the bin. It may feel caring to drop off a meal—and it is, when it's wanted—but often when someone is struggling, a big plate of food is not where they are at. The stress involved in returning all the boxes in which the food came can far outweigh any benefits of the meal (and saying, "No pressure to return the box any time soon" doesn't help—it's still sitting there in the house). And, in some cases, such as when people are recovering from an eating disorder, the act of taking away people's responsibility for their own food preparation can do far more harm than good.

What kinds of requests might we get?

- **Help to shop.** Crowded, noisy places like supermarkets can feel overwhelming. The very act of entering a superstore may trigger a panic attack in those whose anxiety is high. Giving someone who is struggling a lift to a small supermarket at a quiet time of day—or sitting with them as they plan an online delivery—can give them the courage they need to shop for themselves and begin to give their body the nutrition it needs.

- **Help to cook.** Far better than providing meals is spending a few hours with someone cooking together. Making food alongside someone else can be more fun than making food alone. And far better to end up with six wanted meals in the freezer than one unwanted dinner in the bin.

- **Help to pay.** For those whose struggles mean they are unable to work, finances may be very problematic. A church which is willing to give vouchers to spend on food, clothes or school essentials for the children can alleviate much pain. The occasional voucher for something more fun can sometimes be wonderful too! Many churches will also operate a hardship fund that can cover more substantial needs—there may be a significant number of people who need help with fuel and food bills in the coming years.

- **Help to clean.** A dirty home—or garden—is a depressing place to be. A depressed person may find cleaning an impossible task. And so, a downward spiral can begin, resulting in increasing filth and increasing despair. Our instincts might be to pay for a cleaning team to sort it out or to go in and blitz the place ourselves in the hope that the person struggling might be able to then keep things clean. This strategy rarely works. Far better for someone to go round for an hour or two a week and gradually help the person to clear things together with the helper. Encourage and empower the person to do what needs to be done. Someone who struggles with hoarding will find it very hard to let things go—and simply throwing things out will cause immense pain—but together, there may be ways of organising precious possessions and beginning to see that donating a few things brings both freedom and joy.

- **Help to travel.** Appointments can abound. Certainly, if someone needs regular medication reviews or talking therapy, there will be regular travel to be done. Often, when struggling, people can think, "What's the point?" They may find it hard to believe that counselling or medication will make a difference and so find it hard to get motivated to get to meetings across town. If they're reliant on public transport, it might be infrequent or overcrowded, and that makes travel additionally difficult. A lift can make the world of difference. And there may even be some appointments—such as a periodic review with a psychiatrist—where the person struggling may appreciate a friend in the room. And that can help the church understand the aims of the medical professionals as well as helping the medics understand the input of the church better too.

- **Help to write.** In our modern world, one thing is certain: at some point there's going to be an online form to fill out. These can be a nightmare at the best of times, but when life is overwhelming, they can be an insurmountable block. Just sitting with someone as they fill one in can make the impossible possible.

- **Help to exercise.** Getting the body moving is vitally important for those struggling with their mental health. Exercise releases chemicals that promote a sense of wellbeing, relieve stress and enable the body to thrive. But exercise is hard when everything feels bleak. Taking the dog for a walk together, enjoying a cycle ride, going for a jog, throwing a ball or playing a game of football or tennis can provide activity, community and hope.

Sometimes the concern is that these things will take time. And, on one level, they do. But as you scan the list above, you will see that there are ways of combining helping others with doing life yourself. As you take your friend to the supermarket, you can do your own shop; as you encourage your friend to exercise, you keep fit yourself; as you cook batch meals, you can stock your own freezer as well as theirs. Not all acts of practical care need to be additions to our diaries. Those that are additions can be shared around.

Safety and accountability

Safety and accountability, however, are essential. If someone is vulnerable (either in the legal sense or just in the sense that they are finding life desperately hard and could be taken advantage of), it's wise to ensure that anyone helping with money and official forms or having access to their home is in good standing, has an up-to-date police-record check and is overseen by someone in the church.[6] Hidden pastoral care is always unwise. But, with those safety measures in place, practical resourcing is an area which can be shared widely in the congregation.

There may be someone in the congregation who is never going to be a Bible teacher or a formal counsellor, but they do own a friendly dog, and they can easily set aside 45 minutes to take a walk with someone who is finding life hard. There may be someone in the congregation who's not great at talking about Jesus or talking about their feelings but is quite happy to drive someone to the pharmacy to pick up some medication. These will need to be the kinds

---

6 In the UK this is known as a DBS check (Disclosure and Barring Service); different agencies and systems operate in other countries.

of characters that the person struggling is willing to trust, but these examples show that contact and caring roles don't have to land on the shoulders of a few. By sharing these roles, people's diverse gifts can be used in exciting ways, and multiple healthy relationships can begin to form.

It's so important to co-ordinate who is doing what. Sometimes this involves formal structures and people set apart by the church to oversee care (as in Acts 6)—sometimes it can be done more informally. But it's always wise to ensure that someone in leadership is aware of what support is being offered. The church should also ensure that those who are involved in caring for vulnerable people go through the necessary suitability checks.

Giving practical resourcing a chapter of its own like this risks depicting the practical as somehow divorced from the more explicitly Christ-centred conversation in the chapters you've read before. And, sometimes, the people involved in both kids of activity will be very different. But practical resourcing can be explicitly linked to more spiritual care too. A meeting to talk about persevering through the tough times with our eyes on Christ can be combined with a lunchtime bowl of soup. It's fine to spend some of the time cooking, shopping or exercising or talking about sport or the latest TV soap. But truly Christian care will want to be reminding the person who is finding life hard that God loves them and is with them. Practical acts can also be wonderful moments of hope.

Resourcing carers

One group of people who are often overlooked are those who are caring for the more profoundly broken. While most people who struggle with their mental health won't need a formal carer, often there is someone who carries a great deal of responsibility for care. A spouse caring for a depressive partner. A teenager coping with a parent with addictions. A parent in anguish over an anorexic child. Each of them needs the love and caring support of the wider Christian community.

Again, the place to start is to ask what that person needs. The answers may vary widely but often fall into categories like these:

- **A chance to talk.** Carers can become very isolated. The role can be intense and emotionally demanding, and dominate both day and night. Having a small group of people who will check in and ask not how the person struggling is doing but how the person caring is doing can be a breath of fresh air.

- **A chance to pray.** Often carers find it hard to get to church services or small groups—it can be hard to leave the person needing care alone. Offering online access to prayer meetings is a step to inclusion. But facilitating the provision of a prayer triplet (where requests can be shared over the phone and praying done at a time convenient to the carer, not the church calendar) can provide the fuel needed to carry on with eyes on Christ.

- **A chance to rest.** Those caring for image-bearers who are struggling deeply can reach exhaustion levels fast. Offering help to access state-backed or charitable respite services can be useful. Offering funding for a short 24 hours away (or even a trip to the cinema) can bring a smile. Offering two people from the church to come round and sit with the one needing care so the carer can simply have their hair cut without worry can be a blessing.

- **A chance to laugh and praise.** Caring for someone who is in deep despair or finding rational thought hard or prone to lashing out can feel very heavy. Sending links to Christ-centred songs or sharing stories of encouragement—even sending appropriate comedy clips—can bring a smile on a difficult day.

- **A chance to do life with others.** All the ideas in the section about shopping, lifts, exercise, cooking and paperwork apply here too!

And if there are several carers in the congregation, setting up a group where they can offer each other prayer and peer support can be a wonderful encouragement as well.

Resourcing the wider church

Whether or not there are formal carers in the congregation, there will be informal ones. The church is, by its very nature, a place where we care for each other. And it is important to care well for those who are caring well!

That means we will want to check in periodically with people offering care and make sure they are doing ok. It will mean talking with them about whether their serving is sustainable, it will involve ensuring they are still honouring God by taking some rest, and it will include checking in on how their hearts are doing—are they still loving the people they're walking alongside or has a sense of cold duty begun to creep in? Those checks can be in the context of times of prayer. They can be moments of accountability as we gently ensure that the care being given is biblical, safe and wise. They can be conversations where carers can talk over some of the trickier topics, such as boundaries, with someone outside their situation to get an external (and eternal) perspective. And they can be opportunities to thank people for their service—saying how grateful to God we are for their gifts, their humility, their commitment and their care. We will want to have people in the church who are tasked with doing this because, without them, the people walking alongside others will burn out or begin to resent the giving of care.

Along the way, we might want to be signposting people to places where they can get extra training. Books to read, courses and conferences to attend, networks to link with—things that can be done in people's own time to help.

It's a bit like making sure the car has a regular service. Cars can keep running quite happily for years—decades—without anyone doing anything to them. But if you never look under the hood, there's real potential that something deeply serious might be starting to develop. By doing what is practical and wise—ensuring that those walking alongside others are themselves cared for well—we can keep the body of Christ functioning as well as it can. And that is good for everyone involved.

Questions for reflection

1. What structures are in place in your church to ensure people can access practical help in times of need?
2. Think of someone you know who is struggling. What practical act of kindness can you offer this week?
3. Who do you know who is caring long-term for someone? How can you offer to help support them?

CHAPTER 11

COMMON QUESTIONS

This chapter will consider some of the common issues faced by churches seeking to provide wise care for those struggling with their mental health. It will also address a few of the most frequently asked questions.

How do we handle confidentiality?

Even though we won't find the category of confidentiality in Scripture, there is plenty to encourage us to maintain privacy and to avoid gossip.

> *A perverse person stirs up conflict, and a gossip separates close friends.*　　　　　　　　　　　Proverbs 16:28

> *I am afraid that when I come I may not find you as I want you to be, and you may not find me as you want me to be. I fear that there may be discord, jealousy, fits of rage, selfish ambition, slander, gossip, arrogance and disorder.*　　　　　　　　　　2 Corinthians 12:20

There is, rightly, a desire to ensure confidentiality is maintained in regard to issues of health. That is true both of physical and mental health. We want to be in control of who knows what about our health. In medical settings the issue of confidentiality is generally clear and absolute. A doctor who has access to the details of our medical history and current health is not allowed to share it with others, not even our very closest relatives (unless we give permission). In general, this doesn't create too much difficulty, partly because the distinction between professional and patient is so clear.

But church is different. The church is a community with a network of relationships that are both complex and ill-defined. The pastor in your church might be, at one and the same time, your pastor, your friend, your home-group leader, your relative and your car-mechanic (if they happened to be a part-time pastor who tops up their income with a second job). And when a community is complex, the rules for confidentiality are harder to define. Consider this example.

Brad has been diagnosed with depression and admitted to hospital. His wife phones Tom, their church pastor, to pass on this news and asks if the church can pray. In such circumstances, which should Tom do?

- Mention this information to all in church leadership so they can pray.
- Mention this only to "senior leaders" (or paid leaders).
- Send this information out on the church urgent prayer bulletin.
- Mention this at a public prayer meeting.
- Mention it only to Sujit, his senior co-pastor, who has a long-standing relationship with Brad.
- Or should he do none of the above, because Tom only knows what Brad's wife wants and not what Brad wants?

It's tricky. Brad may not be well enough to give an opinion. It may not even be possible to visit or contact him because of temporary restrictions imposed by the psychiatric ward. But suppose Brad was so severely depressed that he was on "suicide watch" with a real concern for his life. Would it be wrong *not* to have people praying in a life-or-death situation? Would it feel strange knowing how differently we would probably respond to a life-or-death situation that involved physical health?

If Brad had been admitted to hospital with acute pancreatitis and was fighting for his life in intensive care, it is hard to imagine we would have the same concerns. Chances are we wouldn't hesitate to act on his wife's request. We would mobilise the church to pray. Presumably, the reason why we respond differently when Brad is depressed is because of the stigma still associated with psychiatric illness. *Yet which should we do?* Resist that stigma by determining to be open about mental illness in the same way we would about physical illness? Or respect the need for more privacy precisely because ignorance and stigma about mental illness persist?

Now let's complicate things still further. Suppose that a week later Brad has improved and texts his friend Sujit (the co-pastor at his church) only to discover that Sujit knows nothing about his illness and hospital admission. Brad is flabbergasted. Didn't his wife let Sujit's co-pastor know? Was this information so unimportant—was he so unimportant—that for a whole week Tom didn't even bother to tell Sujit about it? Brad doesn't feel comforted because the church has a strong confidentiality policy in place. He just feels profoundly disregarded and unloved.

So, what should we do? Here are a few guidelines.

- Wherever possible, **talk explicitly about the way people want their information shared.** Rather than assuming they do (or don't) want others made aware of their illness, we should ask. And include a range of explicit options. If we are thinking of putting something in writing (in a prayer diary or in an urgent prayer bulletin), then send the draft wording to those concerned to make sure they are happy with the way things are described.

- **Don't make unqualified promises of confidentiality**—they are hard to keep and may encourage missteps in relation to safeguarding (see below).
- If your church has some kind of pastoral care team, then it will be important to **think carefully how information will be shared within the team** and how those procedures are communicated to people in the church.

How do we handle safeguarding?

People who struggle with their mental health will, on occasions, present safeguarding concerns. Most commonly this will relate to self-harm and suicide. More rarely, people with mental-health difficulties may present a threat to others. Media coverage tends to give an exaggerated impression of how often mental-health problems result in a threat to others.

Self harm: Self-inflicted harm is a common feature in many types of mental-health difficulty. People who struggle with anxiety, depression or an eating disorder and those diagnosed with certain personality disorders are all prone to self-harm. Sometimes this settles into a pattern in which people inflict superficial cuts on their forearms or legs using razor blades. Self-harm like this can be very problematic ,and people struggling in this way need compassionate and thoughtful care and support. It is a very different problem to that presented by those who are actively suicidal.

Suicide: Both in the UK and the USA, the incidence of completed suicides generally increases with age up to around 45 years of age and then declines (although there is a further increase in the most elderly part of our population). Suicide is three to four times more common among men compared to women.

Many church communities will experience the tragedy of a death by suicide, and churches should be alert to ways of caring for those who experience suicidal thoughts.

One common misunderstanding is thinking that the risk of suicide is increased by asking people about the possibility. There is no evidence, however, that asking about suicidal ideas ever puts the idea into someone's head. On the contrary, asking about suicidal thoughts allows us to identify people at risk and ensure they get the help they need.

Those who provide pastoral care in a church should learn how to ask about suicidal thoughts and what to do if they have concerns about someone's safety. In broad terms, if someone has a specific plan about how they would take their own life, that is a significant risk factor. Having gone further and taken steps to enact that plan (for example, doing some online research into suicide methods or stockpiling drugs) is a still greater concern and will usually require the urgent involvement of mental-health services. In such circumstances, the person at risk should not be left alone until suitable professional help has been obtained.

Risk to others: In situations where there is a concern over risk to others, a specialist safeguarding service should be consulted and their advice followed. That will mean being familiar with your church's safeguarding policy and about lines of accountability. It is important to err on the side of caution. It is better to seek advice and be reassured that you are worrying unnecessarily than not to seek advice and miss something important.

Clearly, wherever pastoral care is being delivered in a church context, safeguarding policies and procedures should be in place locally, and these must always be followed carefully.

The other safeguarding issue to be aware of concerns our own errors and mistakes. If we ourselves are concerned that we may have acted inappropriately in some way, then we should overcome our desire to hide our mistakes and seek advice.

How do I know when to involve others?

Many people with mental-health difficulties are reluctant to seek help and need lots of encouragement before they will do so. However, that is not universally true. Some can seek so much input from others that this itself becomes difficult to manage. Difficulties may arise because multiple people are being consulted and contrary advice is being issued, which becomes confusing. Sometimes individuals who do want to help nevertheless begin to feel overwhelmed by the demands being placed upon them.

An overly anxious parent may be constantly seeking advice about symptoms they have noticed and remedies they have been trying. They may obtain advice from multiple people in the church family, and frequently this leads to people wanting new advice about the advice already given. A deepening muddle of competing opinions all too easily develops.

It generally helps to name this issue with the person concerned. Being clear about what is and is not possible usually helps. This can involve discussing times of the day when you are and are not available and also the total amount of time that you can give. Providing this information will help avoid misunderstandings. It helps ensure that those in need aren't left confused about why help is not forthcoming, and it helps those providing help not to feel guilty because they never seem to be able to give enough.

When someone needs a large amount of support, it will often help to recruit a wider team so that no one person feels as if they have all the responsibility. Sharing the time commitment often works well for those offering help, and it may also prove beneficial for the person requiring help because it helps them learn to manage their requests more appropriately.

What records should I keep?

What represents good practice for record-keeping will vary considerably, both according to local legislation and the context in which care is being given. Where safeguarding concerns exist, it is always important to keep full and confidential records. More usually, record-keeping is something to be done for the benefit of the people we are trying to support. Being able to remember important information will help us to provide the best care and support, and that may mean keeping some kind of notes.

Those notes should be kept securely, and they should be written in such a way that they would be understandable (and acceptable) to the person about whom they are written. GDPR (General Data Protection Regulation, UK) rules will apply in many situations, and it is important that churches are aware of these requirements both in regard to the retention of records and restrictions over the sharing of data with others.

Where a group of people are working together to provide support, good communication between them is so important. It helps to avoid key information getting lost, and it reduces the risk that different things get communicated to the person being supported. Getting mixed messages can be so confusing, and it's important to avoid this. The way the supporting team communicate must, however, be transparent and (to repeat) must be both understandable and acceptable to the person receiving the support.

How do we relate to mental-health professionals?

The issues of confidentiality obviously affect the kind of interactions that will take place with mental-health professionals. In general, unless very specific consent has been granted, it will not usually be possible for any information to be shared by mental-health professionals. This can feel frustrating, but it is obviously important to respect people's privacy.

With mental-health issues, friends and relatives often expect the disclosure of information in a way they never would in other health settings. It is not appropriate to treat everyone with a mental-health problem as though they have lost capacity and need someone to make decisions for them.

In the realm of mental health, few of us will be experts. There will, therefore, be much we do not know. That should not stop us being involved or offering help, but we may need to have a lower threshold for seeking out advice and help from professionals. In a crisis, or when we are simply in doubt about a wise next step, we should be ready to be in contact with a family doctor, mental-health service or sometimes even the police.

One of the best ways to ensure a good exchange of information is for those providing support to attend appointments with the person concerned. Obviously, this should only happen with the person's specific consent, and they must not feel under pressure to agree to this.

Can I do more harm by interfering?

Generally speaking, someone who is asking this question probably isn't going to do any harm. It's those who never even consider this possibility that are more of a worry. It is, of course, important, to know the limits of our knowledge and our competence. But what often lies behind this concern of doing harm is the idea that all mental illness is just too complicated for any untrained person to get involved with.

Yet we would never apply that thinking to people struggling with their physical health. Even though we don't have expertise in the latest chemotherapy regimes, we still want to step toward those undergoing cancer treatment, rather than stay away. And though we may have no knowledge about the arthritic condition that is limiting someone's ability to walk, we would still ask how they are doing and what we can best do to support them.

The same principles can, or should, apply to mental illness. You may not have expertise in anxiety states, but you can offer to accompany someone to church when their fears are preventing them from doing so alone. Nor do we need to understand psychotic illnesses or its treatment to offer practical support to someone struggling to navigate the benefits system.

It probably would be interfering, however, for someone with no expertise to take a dogmatic view about the medication a person is taking or whether or not to take professional advice about a therapy plan. The basic rule is to step toward those in need, but to do so with humility—asking them about their struggles and doing lots of listening rather than lots of advising.

What if someone never seems to get better?

Some mental-health problems are chronic. That doesn't mean they are necessarily worse than others but simply that they last a long time. Some may be lifelong. The same, of course, is true of many physical problems. Certain forms of diabetes and epilepsy and inflammatory bowel disease are, usually, lifelong conditions. They can be controlled by long-term treatment, but usually they are never cured.

Similarly, some of those diagnosed with conditions like schizophrenia, a bipolar disorder or an eating disorder have a lifelong struggle. It is important, therefore, that rather than excluding people from church life because they aren't well, we find ways to involve them. That involvement may need to take account of any limits their mental health may impose, but the same is true for many people with physical difficulties. Responsible churches will build a ramp at the entrance so that people in wheelchairs can gain step-free access. So, if the venue permits, why would we not create a safe, quiet space with an audio feed where people who are anxious can sit and engage with the service away from the crowds which they find create an almost intolerable anxiety?

We should also note that some people with mental-health difficulties find it hard to fit in. Perhaps their social anxiety makes it hard for them to sit with others or causes them to leave midway through a church service. Church communities who are willing to accommodate these things can provide vital support and can help a person build the kind of social network they need. Churches who don't manage this often only contribute to the sense of alienation people feel.

Where possible, rather than limiting people's involvement until they are better', we should try to use people's gifts even when they are struggling. Doing so is such an important way of caring for those whose mental-health issues are long term. A man with long-term mental-health struggles might find social situations almost unbearable, but he might really enjoy driving. Perhaps in a rural church setting, he could serve the 20s and 30s group by taking on the responsibility of driving the church minibus which takes people back to their homes at the end of an evening. Likewise, a young woman who suffered from social anxiety loved being part of the refreshment team in the kitchen to prepare or serve drinks. Having a counter between herself and other people was reassuring, and she was able to build a special bond with the others who helped. It made her feel valued and useful.

How do you help someone who doesn't want to be helped?

It's not unusual to find that people we suspect would benefit from support with mental health don't seem very keen to get it. They may, in fact, be resistant to any suggestion that they have issues with their mental health. This isn't an easy situation to face, but approaching this with a willingness to talk honestly and to explore why someone may be feeling hesitant about such help is an obvious place to start. Fears about the stigma associated with mental-health issues can certainly be a factor and will only reduce as churches speak about these things more openly.

Suggesting a range of options may help reduce the hesitation people feel, as may an offer to go with them when they visit their family doctor. Many online sources of support are available and can provide a stepping-stone to seeking help face to face.

What is the relationship between mental illness and spiritual warfare?

The way in which mental illness and spiritual warfare interact is yet one more subject that deserves far more space than this book allows. These comments provide only the broadest of brush strokes.

The Bible does make connections between sin and suffering. Sin's entry into the world in Genesis 3 brought suffering with it (Genesis 3:14-19). It was the lies of the devil that provided the temptation leading to the fall (Genesis 3:1-5), and it is Christ's victory over evil that will bring the final overthrow of the devil (Revelation 20:10). That day will mean the end of all suffering (Revelation 21:4).

Yet none of this should lead us to make simplistic links between personal sin and suffering. In his comments about the man born blind, Jesus discourages us from thinking that particular suffering should be associated with particular sin. (John 9: 1-3). Neither should we jump to conclusions about a person's mental illness and some specific involvement of the demonic in their condition.

In the present age, evil persists and spiritual warfare is a reality for every Christian believer (Ephesians 6:10-18).

Rightly understood, spiritual warfare is found not merely in extraordinary manifestations of demon possession but in the ordinary battles every believer has with temptation and sin. Moreover, when Jesus expels demons, the gospel accounts describe him as responding not to personal moral evil but to afflictions that need healing (Matthew 4:23-24).

Whenever a believer faces affliction, they are caught up in the reality of spiritual warfare (2 Corinthians 12:7-10; Revelation 2:8-10). This is true in every kind of illness. Those experiencing psychotic illness sometimes talk incessantly about the spiritual realm and the powers of evil. But it should not surprise us that when a person is intensely disturbed and distressed, they refer to the elemental forces of good and evil as a means of expressing their distress. This itself, however, is not an argument for making a simplistic association between demon possession and mental illness.

In such situations our go-to strategy will be to underline the complete and comprehensive victory of Jesus Christ over Satan and all the powers of evil. Reminders of his promise to protect and keep his children will be needed (Psalm 121; John 10:28-29; 17:15; 2 Thessalonians 3:3).

Finally, as with any experience we might have, either of spiritual warfare or mental illness, we should know our limitations and be ready to seek support from others with more experience at an early stage.

For more thinking on this issue, read David Powlison's excellent book *Safe and Sound: Standing Firm in Spiritual Battles.*

SECTION 3:

CARING IN
PRACTICE

SECTION 3

INTRODUCTION

I t's all very well reading a little theory in a book, but what might it look like in practice if we were all to do these things in our local church? What kinds of results might we expect if we put time and effort into resourcing, raising awareness and helping people to relate to others, remember their identity and be refined to be more like Christ?

We certainly won't see perfection—much as we might like to. We could do all the things listed here—and more— and still not see an end to the mental-health struggles in our churches. Only Jesus' return will accomplish that.

We won't see the church becoming experts in all aspects of care. There will always be a place for specialist counsellors— both in parachurch organisations and the secular world.

We won't even necessarily see everybody *wanting* our support—human beings are complex, and there are moments when we all want the help of others and moments when we don't.

But if we pursue Christ and hold out gospel hope to those who already know him—and to those who don't—we will see change.

In this third and final section, we are going to revisit the case studies we set out in chapter 1. And we are going to track through what supporting each of those individuals might look like in an average church—both the encouragements and the discouragements.

These case studies are not being fleshed out to show you how every case of anxiety or depression or addiction will need to be navigated. These are examples—tasters, if you like—of what care might look like. So, reading the case study on anxiety does not give you a template for walking alongside *every* person who struggles with anxiety; it shows you just one of the many ways the principles in this book might work out.

We're aware that what follows is inevitably simplified; there are more twists and turns in real life than we have the time or space to articulate here. But we hope these vignettes put some flesh on the bones and inspire us all to move towards those who are hurting with the love and hope of Christ.

CHAPTER 12

ANXIETY

Remember **Chi**? We met her back in chapter 1. Chi's been a Christian for as long as she can remember. She loves Jesus deeply and wants to serve him with all her life. Every Sunday she's at the service, and every Wednesday she attends her small group, but she rarely says a word. It's not that she doesn't love people or that she has nothing to contribute to discussions about God's word. She is simply scared: utterly paralysed by a fear of getting things wrong or saying something that may upset someone else in the room. At night, she battles panic attacks, gastrointestinal challenges blight her day, and frequently she cries. Life feels so very hopeless—she just doesn't want to be this way.

How might you walk alongside her well?

Understanding Chi

Chi is finding life hard. It's an obvious statement, but it's the best place from which to begin because, by having that reality front and centre in our minds, everything else that follows will be couched in a compassionate concern for a struggling sister. Chi doesn't need *fixing* (she's not a project), nor does she need *rebuking* (there's no wilful sin dominant here), neither does she need simply *affirming* as she is (some affirmation would be good, of course, but some things need to change)—the call is to *love her*, as the Bible commands us to do.

It's not just that Chi is finding things hard; she is finding a *lot* of things hard. She's scared of messing up, scared of people's opinions and scared to simply be in the same room with others. She's scared when it's just her and God too—the nights are no better than the days. That's leading to emotional overload and physical distress. She's exhausted from lack of sleep. Chi's world seems very bleak and lonely and without a clear sense of where to go. It's worth letting the enormity of that sink in. This isn't a young woman making a fuss; she doesn't need to just pull herself together and get over it. This is a huge life-dominating thing for her. And (while the case study isn't explicit about this) it is likely to be fuelled by something deeply painful in the past.

At the moment, Chi is hanging in at church. She's turning up week by week. But, if things don't improve, that probably won't last. The Bible may say that Jesus' burden is light but, at the moment, church is feeling like a 10-ton weight. And no one can bear that long term.

She needs help. But where will she turn? And what will she receive?

Chi and the wider world

It's to be expected that Chi will be encouraged by friends to speak with her doctor. And doing so could be helpful and wise. After an assessment, and possibly a referral to specialist services, it is probable that she would be diagnosed with generalised anxiety disorder, or possibly with something like a social anxiety disorder. This is a diagnosis that is marked by fear of situations where a person is open to the scrutiny of others, and where that fear has been present for six months or more and tends to lead to distress, avoidance or costly endurance of social situations. Such a diagnosis describes her ongoing battle well. She finds it hard to use her voice when there are other people around.

The doctors may suggest some medication that might help. An antidepressant might lift her mood—an anti-anxiety drug might take the edge off the panic and fears. Doctors might refer her for an online relaxation course or 12 weeks of cognitive behavioural therapy to help her reframe her experience of being in a crowded room. She may be advised to join a gym—exercise can be helpful—or try meditation. And she will no doubt be given plenty of encouragement along the way. All such things might be of great use.

But what about the church?

Helping Chi by raising awareness

It's entirely likely that Chi feels as if she is the only one at church that struggles in this way. As she looks round the congregation, she sees people who are happy to speak up—and, indeed, quite a few that never seem to stop sharing their views. She wonders if she's a "bad Christian"—someone who is struggling because her faith is unusually weak. She suspects that others are doubting her commitment or her knowledge because she never prays out loud or contributes in Bible studies.

At the end of another tough Sunday gathering, she decides that coffee time feels too hard. She heads for the bookstall instead. Her eyes glide past the biographies ("People better than me" she assumes). She toys with some commentaries. And then she sees them—three books, side by side, on anxiety. She takes one off the shelf. As she reads the back cover, she notices the statistics. To her surprise, it seems that anxiety is pretty common in the Christian world. With eyebrows raised, she replaces it on the shelf and wonders if she might not be the only one. She glances at the second book—there's a section there on God's compassion. In the third, she sees the offer of strategies, and she resolves to give reading it a go. The very presence of those books has given her hope.

As she walks towards the church door, a friend catches

her eye. She's smiling. "I've read that book too," she says. "But you don't struggle with anxiety," Chi replies. "Oh, I do," comes the reply. The ensuing conversation is short; there's no sense in which it makes everything better, but suddenly Chi knows that she is not alone. A friend has given a glimpse of her struggles and allowed herself to be known. Awareness has been raised. Anxiety is safe to discuss in this church. Believers here know that life hurts but are confident that there's a way through.

It's the best Sunday Chi has had at church in years.

Helping Chi relate

Chi probably isn't going to open up about her struggles in her small group—that's the very place where it's hardest to utter a word. The conversation to come will need to be on a much smaller scale. An invitation to coffee, somewhere where she feels safe, from a sister in Christ she trusts (or feels she can learn to trust) is ideal.

The conversation is stilted at first, but she's impressed that her friend isn't fazed by the silences. She appreciates that there's no barrage of questions but a much more open suggestion: "Tell me a little of what it's like to be you". It's a freeing question. She can talk as little or as much as she likes without pressure for more. And there's no fear of getting the answer wrong. She can let people into her world and let them see the pain.

There's no sense that this meeting is to "fix the problem" of her silence midweek. Her lack of contribution to the group is not even mentioned—which she's relieved about because that would have just left her feeling condemned. It's a conversation in which two women get to know each other. It's to get to understand what makes her tick, and to build some foundations for future conversations to come.

A date is put in the diary to meet again. Chi's excited; this could be the start of something lovely. She's not naïve—she might have a panic attack later about the fact that she didn't say something as well as she could have, but there's nothing new there. Overall, what happened in that conversation felt good.

A week or two later, there's another meeting, another coffee and another conversation. A little more exploration of life. And then a deeper question comes. "How do you think God sees you?"

It's an opinion question, not one with a right or wrong answer. That makes it easier for her to speak her mind. It doesn't prevent the phrases from getting stuck in her throat, but it's possible to squeeze out a word. "Disappointed—he's disappointed in me." That is her firm belief.

It's tempting for her friend to jump in with "No, that's not true—he loves you". But, with Chi, that would just shut the conversation down. A response like that would scream, "You opened your mouth. You got it wrong, again. There's no point in you talking at all." Instead, her friend wisely follows up with another question: "How can you engage with him more about that?"

There will come a moment when Chi's eyes will need to rest on Bible passages that reorientate her thinking. We must not forget that Chi's views of God and herself aren't quite right. But we can put them on short-term hold while we work on some more foundational things. Chi doesn't find using her voice easy; the best place to start practising using her voice is in her relationship with God. By learning to speak with God, she will learn to speak with others—and when she is able to speak with others, she will be able to speak about the things that need to change.

Over the weeks that follow, her friend invites Chi to read a variety of psalms and see the kinds of phrases that David and other authors use. Chi is shocked—the psalms, in places, are pretty raw. Chi had always been under the impression that any words you used in conversation needed to be carefully crafted to appease or please the recipients' ears. Little by little, Chi starts to pray with the same earthiness and honesty that she has been reading in the words of David. Initially, it's hard. There are lingering feelings of guilt at "speaking out of turn" to God. But those psalms… the precedent is there.

Helping Chi remember her identity

It's a few weeks into one-to-one conversations and new ways of trying to pray, and Chi is learning that using her voice need not be a terrifying thing. At small group, she's even started saying "amen" at the end of other people's prayers—and with a hearty tone as well.

Her friend returns to the conversation where Chi said that God is disappointed in her. She asks why Chi thinks that is. After a pause, she utters, "Because I'm not like everyone else". The pair of them flip to Ephesians 1. Chi's pulse begins to quicken—she doesn't want to say something wrong. But her friend defuses the tense moment: "Let's just sit back and hear from our heavenly Dad." She reads out Paul's words.

> *Praise be to the God and Father of our Lord Jesus Christ, who has blessed us in the heavenly realms with every spiritual blessing in Christ. For he chose us in him before the creation of the world to be holy and blameless in his sight. In love he predestined us for adoption to sonship through Jesus Christ, in accordance with his pleasure and will—to the praise of his glorious grace, which he has freely given us in the One he loves. In him we have redemption through his blood, the forgiveness of sins, in accordance with the riches of God's grace that he lavished on us.* Ephesians 1:3-8

"That's you," she says at the end. "That's you and me in all our diversity; that's what God thinks." Her friend doesn't pose a question. She doesn't want this to revert to a situation where Chi is worried about getting the interpretation wrong. She leaves a silence. Chi fills it in the end. "Can that really be how God sees me?"

Her friend suggests they work through a bit of a Gospel together. No tough questions: just a chance to observe what they see. And that's what they do over the next few weeks. Left to her own devices—and able to prepare in advance— Chi's insights are a delight. She easily picks up on the goodness and sovereignty of Christ. Her face lights up as she sees the complete messes that Jesus calls to follow him. She mulls for days over the way Jesus gently restores those who have gone astray. As the months go on, she begins to see that this God, while holy, isn't terrifying. His standards may be high, but he doesn't wield them like a big stick to knock his followers flat. This is the Father whose arms are open wide. And Chi is reassured to know that she can be messy alongside the rest of the messy people in church.

Helping Chi be refined

It's taken months to get to this point, but the foundations for change are now secure. She is established in solid, honest and committed relationships in the church family. She is starting to see more clearly her true identity in Christ. This is the point where a new question can be introduced. "In what ways would you like to change to be more like Christ?"

In response to the question, her friend is astonished to hear her say that she has a list! For Chi, the previous weeks have thrown into sharp relief where things are not as they should be, and not as they could be. And in the security of the relationship she has developed, she now feels able to articulate them all. Unsurprisingly, the first one on the list is the desire to be able to walk into a group setting and speak.

She texts her small group and asks them to pray. She knows she'll need people on their knees for the journey to come. She also asks them not to ask her lots of questions about how it's going. She knows that, at this stage, she won't be able to cope. It's a big step—in that one act she's already begun to use her voice.

In the quietness of her heart—and in conversations with her friend—she begins to tease out the difference between *personality* and *participation*. It's ok to be quiet, but God still wants her to join in with community life. She looks at the gift lists in the Bible and, together with her friend, thinks that maybe giving and wisdom are where her gifts lie. Instantly, that opens up opportunities to use those gifts as someone else in the group is struggling to put food on the table. She's already getting more embedded in the community without saying a word.

She finds herself wanting to pray for the person in need though. Her prayers gradually become a bit freer. That spurs her on to venture the occasional "How's it going?" over coffee time after church.

As she begins to see good fruit forming in her life, she identifies a key area to address. She often thinks to herself, "My words don't matter," and she starts to understand that that's an "old self" thought, not a "new self" one. She resolves to catch it every time it pops into her head. Little by little she brings that thought to the Lord in prayer and asks him to change her heart. She reads Song of Songs and sees how people who love each other delight to hear each other's voices. She dips into 2 Kings 5—if God could use the words of a slave girl to bring about good, then maybe, in Christ, there's hope for her too. Gradually her mind is transformed. She dwells on the equipping work of the Spirit. And after a while, she's able to say this prayer: "Thank you, Lord, that my words do matter, because you have designed me to use my words to your glory. Help me to use them well." It takes time. But step by step she begins to change.

It's an exciting day when it first happens. She's been wise and asked the small group leader if she can have the passage and questions in advance. But with a flutter in her heart, she does it—she ventures an opinion in the small group. It's a brilliant insight, and the rest of the group praise God.

Helping Chi with some practical resources

Along the way, Chi's friends rally round in wonderful ways. They invite her out for "anti-socials" (where they sit in a café together and just read books in silence). It helps her get used to the company of others without the pressure of having to speak. They text her Bible verses of encouragement. They ask her to dog-sit when they go away. (There's nothing quite like a mad spaniel to get you chatting with ease.) And they help her plan what she's going to say to the doctor when the next appointment comes round.

Chi will never become an extrovert. Why would she? She's just not wired that way. She continues to struggle with anxiety—her journey is not over yet—but it doesn't paralyse her anymore, at least not every day. She's knows she's loved, safe and able to use her voice for the good of those around—and that's a precious place to be.

CHAPTER 13

DEPRESSION

We met **Andy** in chapter 1 too. He is young, single, intelligent and doing well in his career. Normally, he's the life and soul of the Bible-study group—always cracking jokes, offering to help or organising social events. But things haven't seemed quite right in recent months. It's been a gradual thing, but he's been noticing less energy, less enthusiasm and a kind of gloominess that just isn't like him. Despite having many friends, Andy feels increasingly alone. A natural self-confidence is giving way to darker thoughts about being a failure and having let everyone down. The early mornings are the worst. Sleep is elusive, and lying in the darkness he can genuinely believe he's unlovable and without value, and that the world would be a better place without him. His thoughts get very bleak then, and a cursory glance at his tablet search history would show that he has recently begun to explore how people go about ending their lives.

How might you walk alongside him well?

Understanding Andy

One of the difficulties with Andy is the mismatch between the way people think of him and the person he is increasingly becoming. This shift from a normal, sociable and outgoing person to someone locked into despairing and depressive dread is a big jump. And most of the time even Andy himself doesn't want to admit this is happening to him. He certainly does his best to hide it from others.

Indeed, the feelings of failure that are associated with his ever-lower mood only serve to persuade him that he must hide what is really going on.

Guilt, shame, despair and hopelessness are prominent elements in Andy's experience. But he is a sufficiently well-taught Christian to know that he isn't supposed to feel like this. Hasn't the gospel covered our shame, dealt with our guilt and provided us with a sure hope? What possible reason can there be for wallowing in shame and guilt and all the rest, then? But simply telling himself that these feelings aren't allowed doesn't seem to make any difference. He feels them just the same. Andy can even feel guilty about feeling guilty and ashamed of feeling shame. Sometimes it seems to him that he is lost in a fog without the faintest idea of how to move forward. Feelings drag him down, and he lacks the energy to resist them. This inability to "pick himself up" and "be his normal self" only compound his sense of uselessness.

Perhaps worst of all are the feelings of hopelessness. He can't bring himself to imagine that this is ever going to change. Just as he has no idea where these thoughts and feelings have come from, he has no idea how or why they might ever go away. And the thought of being stuck with this level of despair and hopelessness for ever is utterly unbearable. That's why darker thoughts kick in—why ending it all begins to seem like the only way out. Part of him knows such thoughts make no sense, and that's what prevents him from mentioning them to anyone else. But at other times the idea that there is at least one way out of this oppressive gloom is a strange kind of comfort. And in an odd kind of way, it has become the only remaining "hope" that he has.

Andy and the wider world

Andy has never been one to visit his doctor much. And the idea of doing so now isn't at all appealing. What would he say? How would he explain himself? Andy himself can't really make sense of what's going on. How could he explain it to someone else? And besides which, right now doing anything new is a challenge—especially anything that requires initiative and brings any degree of social challenge. So in this, as in many other situations, inertia wins the day.

It surprises him sometimes how few people seem to notice. He has pulled out of family gatherings, but his parents assume he's busy with work and church. Text messages from friends have gone unanswered, but if they follow up at all, it is generally with irritation rather than concern. They feel the onus is on him to be in touch with them now.

Andy hadn't really considered using the language of "depression" to describe what was happening until he read a newspaper article about a famous sportsman who suffered from depression for many years. The description did seem to fit, and that led to him exploring depression online. He discovered a whole mix of things. There were lots of articles about biochemistry and serotonin. Plenty of accounts of people whose lives had been restored by taking antidepressants. Confusingly, however, others seemed to take a much more negative slant on antidepressants, and there were many references to "excessive over-prescribing". There were even some alarming accounts of people who experienced severe side effects or long-lasting withdrawal symptoms.

Other people seemed to encourage simple self-help remedies. Exercise, better diet and regular sleep all featured prominently. And then there were recommendations for everything from St John's Wort and light boxes all the way through to cold-water swimming and herbal teas. None of that seemed very helpful to Andy. Recommending sleep was particularly unhelpful. He *couldn't* sleep—and that was the very problem. And he had neither the energy nor the enthusiasm to shop for himself, never mind cook. As for a new exercise regime—that felt like asking him to climb Everest.

His internet searches left him uncertain and confused. Some people clearly saw depression as a disease to be fixed with a pill. At one level that seemed reassuring—because perhaps this wasn't his fault after all. But mostly he found it incomprehensible—because surely he was responsible for the way he felt. He also found it to be at odds with his faith—because if he really believed what he claimed to believe, surely he wouldn't feel like this.

Helping Andy by raising awareness

The mix of inertia and isolation that Andy feels certainly creates an unhappy dynamic with church. At times he feels that people simply can't be bothered with him, and that can make him feel a little cross. But more often he feels so wretched that others ignoring him seems entirely appropriate. What he doesn't have is any sense that his church could ever understand what he is going through. When hands are raised during worship songs that describe joy and hope, he feels more alienated than ever.

So it takes him entirely by surprise when the notice sheet announces a church meeting on the subject of depression. A Christian psychiatrist has been invited to speak, and the evening is billed as being suitable for the whole church family "to help us be a church that better understands depression and is more able to help those who struggle". He hadn't expected that. He assumed that other Christians would be dismissive, perhaps even critical, of anyone who struggled with depression.

It still takes enormous effort to get to the evening event. And he is filled with dread. Will people know why he's there? Will they ask him questions? It turns out to be fine. There isn't much conversation in groups, and he is careful to arrive late and leave quickly at the end. During the evening there is a mix of biological information (not all of which he understands), spiritual reflection (not all of which he agrees with) and mention of all sorts of treatment options (most of which he's never heard of). But in some ways the content really didn't matter. What matters is that his church has put this event on in the first place. It says something profoundly important. It means they recognise this thing called "depression" and that he is, somehow, allowed to struggle in this way. It makes it possible to imagine talking to someone.

Two things that are said that evening stick in his memory. One is that *depression can affect anyone*. And the second is that every person's experience of depression is unique. There isn't a one-size-fits-all description. It really helps to hear that, because now he feels that if he did speak to someone, perhaps they wouldn't think he was a failure or a fraud or both.

Perhaps the very best part of the evening came during question time at the end. One man asking a question said he believed that depression was "simply a sin and that Christians who found themselves feeling low just needed to repent and pull themselves together". This statement was firmly and articulately squashed by the speaker, who said thinking that way was the reason why churches were so often such difficult places for people with depression, and that God called us to show compassion and care instead.

Helping Andy relate

That closing comment about compassion and care was probably the trigger that persuaded Andy that he should try and open up about what was going on. But it still wasn't clear who he should talk to. Saying something in the context of his home group was definitely a step too far. Even approaching his home-group leaders felt too difficult. The senior pastor might, he supposed, have some expertise, but he always seemed so busy. Then a couple of weeks after that evening, the church announced that it was launching a new intensive pastoral-care team. The aim of the team was to provide support to those with more complex pastoral problems, and those in the team had received some training to help with this.

All it required was an email contact, and they would follow up. That made it all seem very manageable, and within a week or two Andy found himself describing his experience to Brian, who, it turned out, worked for a local mental-health charity. Brian was confident and patient, and that made Andy feel safe to talk. It took some time to describe things, but Brian listened patiently.

Several things happened after that. First, Brian encouraged Andy to visit his doctor to get proper medical advice. Brian even offered to give Andy a lift to the surgery to provide support. Second, Brian encouraged Andy to speak to his home-group leaders, and when Andy looked apprehensive, Brian asked if it might help if they did that together. Brian also asked permission to tell the senior pastor about Andy's depression so that he and others on the staff team could be praying for him. That all felt both supportive and encouraging.

None of this took Andy's depression away. But for the first time in quite a while, Andy had a small sense of hope. People were with him in his struggle. Moreover, Brian said he had known many other Christians who had been depressed and who had recovered. Andy couldn't imagine ever feeling better again, but it helped to know that Brian believed things could change.

The regular meetings with Brian helped Andy find words for what was happening to him. That made it easier to talk to others. Things that had previously defied description could now be shared with others in the home group and even with one of his colleagues at work—all of which lessened his sense of isolation and made going to work and church and social events just a little bit more possible.

Helping Andy remember his identity

Brian suggested to Andy that they might read a book together. It provided a Christian perspective on depression. At first, reading was too much, so Brian provided an audio copy which Andy could listen to. They would read small sections and discuss them. There were two things that Andy found particularly helpful. One was the range of factors involved in depression. Andy started to see himself through the lens of the gospel—as someone made in the image of God but living in a fallen world. He began to see how affected he was, like everyone else, by his sinful nature as well as all the things going on in his physical body. It helped Andy see just how many different factors were involved in his depression. The second thing that helped was the idea that in depression a kind of vicious cycle was operating which meant that a lower mood led to decreased social interaction which led to a still-lower mood, and so it went on.

But the really striking material came in the conversations he had with Brian about the spiritual dynamic operating in depression. When Brian showed him psalms that so obviously reflected his own experience, Andy was amazed. How had he never noticed those before? God had chosen to include in the Bible the words of believers struggling with despair and shame and guilt and hopelessness—*just like him*. That made such a difference. It didn't immediately fix anything, but it did give his experience a kind of validity. For the first time Andy felt able to speak to God about the feelings he was experiencing and call on him for help.

Brian also encouraged Andy to explore some Old Testament stories that engaged with experiences of hardship and struggle.

They read the book of Ruth together, and Andy was struck by this story of a woman who felt abandoned and hopeless, and yet through whom God was achieving great things. Naomi may not have known the significance of the child born to her daughter-in-law, but we do. And it helped to see God working in secret ways even in the deepest hardship.

The cumulative effect of their reading and conversations together was to help Andy develop a sense that severe hardship and even despair didn't mean God had abandoned him. Believers did, at times, walk through the darkest valley and yet, in the words of Psalm 23, God was still with them, and in that there was comfort. He realised that he could honour God by demonstrating faith even in depression—and that gave him hope.

Helping Andy be refined

As the very worst of the darkness eased and a few shafts of light began to break through, Andy found he began to reflect a little on his experience. He realised that he wasn't trying to return to "normal". It began to occur to him that there were some things that God was teaching him through this period of trial. One concerned his own sense of self sufficiency. He had prided himself on his ability to cope, and that meant he generally kept others at arm's length. That had changed. The support he got from Brian and the realisation of his own limitations had given him a new sense of what church was supposed to be. He wasn't sure he would ever have understood these things had the depression not hit.

There were also qualities in Jesus that mattered more to him now. Brian had been compassionate and patient, and the care he'd shown him was profoundly steadfast. He realised that these were reflections of Christ, and Andy wanted to show more of these qualities in his own life too.

This life story could, of course, have taken a different

path. Andy's depression might not have lifted, and he could have been someone who wrestled with depression long-term. That brings different challenges. To others in the church, it would bring the responsibility of sticking with Andy for the long haul: to provide love and care and to speak words of hope and comfort even when they don't seem to be making any difference. It also brings the challenge of, rather than waiting until he is "better", finding ways that Andy can be involved in community life and service even while depression presses in. That will be part of his growth and will bring refining not just to him but also to the wider body of Christ.

Helping Andy with some practical resources

At his lowest ebb, Andy didn't have energy for much. Even conversation was often beyond him. At that point, giving Andy a lift to home group or church on a Sunday was vital. It kept him involved. Brian also agreed a safety plan with Andy that could be put into action if his thoughts of self-harm ever seemed to be getting out of control.

When reading was too much, an audio Bible helped, as did the audio version of that book on depression. When he felt ready for it, reading accounts of the way others had struggled with depression was also helpful.

Andy was also grateful for the times that Brian helped him join in with a work party doing some DIY on the church building. He felt useful, he felt involved and it meant being with others in a context where he wasn't having to talk.

A year or more later, he can't really recapture just how the depression made him feel, but he can remember the way others supported him, and from that experience he has learnt to demonstrate a patience and care in his interactions with others that weren't natural for him before. Andy will never forget that.

CHAPTER 14

ADDICTION

Possibly you know someone like **Siobhan**—an occasional attender at church, at best. Her life is chaotic, marred by the abuse she has experienced past and present, the pain of which she dampens with whatever she can afford. Every day there's alcohol; her flat is littered with empty bottles and the cheap corner-shop bags in which they came. Some days there's cash for drugs—cannabis, or occasionally heroin if she's been able to beg, borrow or even steal from family or friends. When she's sober, she loves reading God's word and praying. There have been so many times when she's tried to get clean. But the bottle always seems to trump the Bible in the end. Most people gave up on her long ago.

How might your church walk alongside her?

Understanding Siobhan
People like Siobhan tend to draw strong emotions from those who meet her. Some overflow with compassion for an image-bearer who is so obviously "broken". Others find themselves convinced that God is able to help her—but don't want to get personally involved. The third group often has the loudest voice—they're the ones who think she's beyond helping. Convinced that Siobhan is her own worst enemy, they say the church shouldn't pour any more resources into someone who "clearly" doesn't want to help themselves.

God sees her with different eyes. Her life may be chaotic, but she is a believer. She is lavished with grace. God loves her—he sees her as forgiven, free and family. The Lord rejoices over her with singing (Zephaniah 3:17). Obviously, God is aware that her addiction is still alive and that there is much change needed in her life. But that doesn't alter the fact that she is a child of God and an essential part of the body of Christ. She's struggling, but she is still a saint who, in love, has been chosen, and who is called to love others in return.

Before going any further, it's worth reflecting on what's good in her story. She loves God's word; she knows her Bible well. And she is quick to turn to her Father in prayer—there's no reluctance to repent or to acknowledge her need of the one who knows her best. There is a desire to follow Jesus in the complexity of life. She has tried to get clean. This isn't a woman who thinks her addiction is no problem; she longs to be free of it. She gets to church sometimes. And she longs to be like Jesus, on her sober days at least.

And it's not surprising she is struggling a great deal. Her life has been a catalogue of pain. Abused throughout her childhood by family members and friends, she has been repeatedly beaten, raped and bombarded with cruel words. She wasn't ever encouraged to attend school—she has no qualifications to her name. She was first given drugs by an older half-sibling when she was ten and was addicted by her early teens. Drugs weren't a choice for her at the start, and now, after years of use, they've taken a terrible toll on her body. When she does try to get clean, the withdrawal symptoms are hard to bear. She's still living in an abusive environment—that a husband who alternates lavish words with lashing out. She's in near constant physical and emotional pain from his wounds. But other than him, she's pretty much alone. Most of her other friends aren't able to handle her stories of suffering—or the requests for cash.

It's inescapable that she has made some deeply unwise

choices along the way. She continues to choose to numb the immense pain of her life rather than address some of the issues that underlie it. At times her activities are not just unwise but criminal, and that simply is not right. When she's desperate, she lies—to her family, neighbours or anyone who'll hear. There are moments when she turns her back on the Lord and deliberately walks away from his will. There are certainly many Sundays when she prioritises cider over church community. Such things we cannot condone.

Set out like this, though, maybe we see her in a more nuanced light than our first instincts may have led us to assume. She's not all sinner; she's not all sufferer; she's not all saint. She's a mix. And so are we.

Siobhan and the wider world

Siobhan is likely to have a posse of professionals who know her well—from doctors to police. She's a regular visitor to her doctor's surgery—her health has been failing for years. She's been an outpatient at the local psychiatric unit many times as she's tried to get clean. She's been on methadone as well as antidepressants and mood stabilisers. She's tried psychotherapy, hypnosis, mindfulness, CBT. She's known at Alcoholics Anonymous and Narcotics Anonymous—she's taken part in group therapies galore. But there's little that's active right now. She's been through all the options multiple times and is now being monitored. Everyone suspects her story won't end well.

She is seen by her neighbours as a problem. She's laughed at by some of the local kids. There's a small group of people with whom she can drink or get high—and sometimes she feels they're close, but there are plenty of arguments too. Her reputation is that she is someone who can be lovely but can be hard to get alongside,

Even with hearts full of compassion, it might be hard to

see how the church can really help Siobhan, and it's important to be clear that medical supervision of withdrawal from the alcohol and drugs will be essential if she ever tries to get clean again. But here there is still so much we can do.

Helping Siobhan by raising awareness

She's grown up with violence, alcohol and drugs. Siobhan doesn't need to know information about their snare—she is an expert. Most of the people she mixes with are users, so she's not under any impression that she's the only one. But she thinks she's the only one at church, and that's often why she doesn't go. Much as she sees Jesus as the "friend of sinners", she sees church as a place where only the good and respectable gather. As far as she's concerned, she doesn't really fit on a Sunday. And she fears that others look down on her when she's there.

A book is unlikely to be of help—reading has never really been her thing. But she listens to the prayers spoken in church services with great intent. One Sunday, as her eyes are closed, her heart suddenly skips a beat. The person leading the prayers says this: "Father, please bless all those in our congregation struggling with anger, abuse or addiction". Really? "All those in the congregation"—could that be true? Is this church genuinely a place where multiple addicts come. At the end of the service, she approaches the minister. "How many addicts come to this church?" "Many" comes the reply. Some are addicted to alcohol or drugs, others to gambling or porn, still others to the toxic lure of approval or control.

Siobhan smiles. She's encouraged to hear that she's not alone. She's intrigued by the range of addictions cited. There's something right about acknowledging that many of us have an insatiable craving for something that we think will give us what we need. She's encouraged that the minister sees this. In that single act of someone praying for addicts in her church, she suddenly gets new hope that helps her get along on Sundays just a little bit more.

As she comes along, she begins to discover that there's a Bible-centred course about to start to help promote change. The leaders emphasise that regular attendance is needed and promise to call for her an hour before the start of the course each week to increase the chances of her getting along. They manage her expectations: a few weeks looking at her heart through a biblical lens probably isn't going to change everything, but it can help change a bit. She's keen to give it a go.

Helping Siobhan relate

She's burned a few bridges over the years. Some congregation members who have tried to help in the past have become exhausted or have lent her money that has not come back. She feels ashamed. They are rightly cautious about getting used again. Boundaries are going to be important: no one is going to lend her cash, no one is going to leave their bags unattended in the group, and no one is going to meet her one-to-one, but always in twos, for the safety of all involved. There will be boundaries on time, on energy, on resources— but no boundaries on love or grace. This is a sister in Christ, and she is desperately in need of kindness and care.

A group of six people agree to help come alongside her. Two are the leaders of her small group. Two are going to "do life" with her—walking, shopping, talking and fun. They'll pray with her too—and are looking forward to learning more about prayer from Siobhan and the open way in which she frequently turns to the Lord. Two are going to respond to any requests for practical help; they won't impose their agenda on her but will happily help her explore housing options, rehab options, accessing the local food bank and more. Some are people who have known—and liked—Siobhan for years. Some are going to get to know her bit by bit. It's a bit more artificial than letting friendships naturally grow, but there are some complexities here and Siobhan gets that. She understands her past actions mean the church wants to be wise.

It's important that there's group communication, and Siobhan knows that too. If the six are to be consistent, they'll need to check in regularly with each other because Siobhan has been known to pit people against each other in the past. They'll also want to be praying together for her and for each other. Prayer is the bedrock of any pastoral care. It's important too that, while these relationships might be slightly contrived at the start, they aim to grow towards something more organic and real. The aim is not to morph friends into volunteers but to help volunteers gradually become friends.

Helping Siobhan remember her identity

There's probably not going to be anything more important than helping Siobhan see herself and her world through the lens of Christ. She is acting like a mess because she genuinely believes she is a mess. She is hurting herself and allowing herself to be hurt because that is what she believes she deserves, or that there is no alternative. There can be a temptation to focus on the call to holiness (and a little later, that will certainly have its place) but, for now, asking Siobhan to stay sober will feel about the same as asking a fish to stop swimming in water and start walking on land. The key to making that possible is that she starts to have a growing awareness that, in Christ, she is designed to be free.

But isn't she a Christian? Yes, but one that's stuck in the "gospel gap". She knows she's forgiven—she is looking forward to heaven—but she doesn't yet understand how the gospel changes her now. Her friends speak with her about the woman who met Jesus at the well in John 4. It's a story Siobhan has loved for years. They read it as Siobhan listens, and they ask her what makes her love it so much. "The fact that Jesus would talk to someone that everyone else thought was a mess," comes the reply. They encourage her to reflect on the end of the story. How did this woman's interactions with Jesus change her relationship with the community? "It brought them together again." That's our aim: for Siobhan to encounter Jesus in such a way that she knows she is his, and knows that so deeply that she will want to move back towards her church family and neighbourhood knowing she can be different.

In order to achieve that well, she is likely to benefit from teasing out how active Jesus is in the here and now. She's aware he's present and loving and forgiving, but she's never really dwelt much on things like his leading, transforming, protecting attributes. Psalm 23 is a safe place to begin. Over a period of months, her friends help her explore what it means to live life with a Shepherd. What does protection look like (especially for someone who is being abused)? What does provision look like, and how does God provide? How is he leading her? Where is he leading her to? What are her responsibilities along the way? Each conversation varies in length from a few minutes to a couple of hours. Sometimes there are two in a week; sometimes she goes "off grid" for a while. But gradually she begins to see how beautiful it is not just to know Jesus but to follow him—confident that the Spirit is equipping her to do so each day.

Helping Siobhan be refined

The topic of shame comes up a lot. She knows she is objectively forgiven for what she has done, but she still feels tainted by what has been done to her. Abuse leaves a legacy of scars. Somehow it always feels as if there's a bit of the abuser's dirt lingering in the soul. She agrees to try to change one thought: the one that goes, "You'll always be a mess". She knows that's not what her Shepherd sees. Each time she thinks it, she quickly catches it and acknowledges that it's at odds with what the Bible says. She asks for God's help to see herself differently. She asks for forgiveness for those moments when she's acted as if she is nothing but mess. And she spends time praying that she will stop believing the words that have been spoken over her by abusive men all her life. She reads Ephesians 1, the stories of Rahab and Tamar—and more. She dwells on the person of the Spirit and the promise of Philippians 1:6.

> *... that he who began a good work in you will carry it on to completion until the day of Christ Jesus.*

With help, she digs into what it means for Jesus to have broken the power of sin when he died and rose again—not just the sin we have done but the power of the sin done to us too. And slowly she begins to put on the new self: to see that she is forgiven and free.

There's no rose-tinted mirror here. By taking off the thought process that she will always be a mess, she's not replacing it with some fantasy that she's fine as she is. But hope is being injected. God is a God of change—the possibility is real.

Helping Siobhan with some practical resources

Along the way, Siobhan enjoys cook-ins with friends. She's actually a good cook when she sets aside the time. She appreciates lifts to appointments; she's started seeing her psychiatrist more regularly as a result, and she's beginning to ponder the possibility of trying to get clean again. One of the older members of the congregation is beginning to find it hard to get out and about—and so Siobhan, along with other friends, joins a work party to help clear some of the garden weeds. It's the first time she's been able to serve others in years. And she loves the sense of purpose and the large quantities of giggles it brings. She's discovered that people can be safe, the outdoors is fun—and that she has a minor fear of worms. And she couldn't be happier about all three.

Have we helped? Siobhan is still an addict. She is still in an abusive relationship. Over the years, the church can help her break free of both. But she's already engaged in astonishing growth. She's more connected to her church community, she's seeing God more clearly, seeing herself more biblically, tasting the real possibility of Christ-centred change and beginning to enjoy purpose in service. It's unlikely to be a linear improvement from here (it isn't for anyone), but she's on an upward trajectory and, in Christ, there's a genuine possibility that she can live abuse- and alcohol-free.

CHAPTER 15

PSYCHOSIS

Every now and then we meet someone like **Ben**. He's been ill since his early 20s—which is when the voices started and his grip on reality seemed to ebb away. His parents remain supportive, and he usually joins them at church, but at times it's been extraordinarily difficult. When his psychotic symptoms are acute, Ben's convinced that he's Jesus—reincarnated and with new revelations to share. Even when things are calmer, he still struggles to order his thoughts and to locate himself reliably in reality. Medication helps, but it has side effects, and these make him reluctant to take it. He finds it hard to sit still so often paces at the back of the service and then wanders out for a cigarette before coming back in. Ben sometimes attends a small group, but expressing himself is difficult. He either dominates with inappropriate expressions of his delusional beliefs or sits looking distracted as if his thoughts are elsewhere. People want to love him well, but they don't know how to.

Understanding Ben

Our churches often have very few people with any first-hand experience of supporting people who suffer from psychotic illness. It's not that psychosis is all that rare. Schizophrenia affects around 1% of the general population and psychotic symptoms can also develop in people diagnosed with conditions such as bipolar disorder, postpartum psychosis, and sometimes in severe depression.

Psychosis is a term used to describe some of the more severe forms of mental illness. There is considerable variation in the way that people are affected, but a disturbed grasp on reality is generally a central feature. That can involve both disordered thoughts and disturbed perceptions. Delusions are false beliefs which are held contrary to reasonable judgement. In Ben's case that can include the belief that he is Jesus and that God communicates with him through secret signals hidden within programmes on the TV. When he is most unwell, he believes Satan is using the police and the medical profession to try and stop him from fulfilling his ministry. That, as you might imagine, often prevents him accepting the professional help that he needs.

Disordered perceptions take the form of hallucinations— perceptions that don't correspond with any actual external event. In Ben's case that generally involves him hearing voices. To him, they aren't voices in his head. They sound just the same as the voices he hears when people actually talk to him. But the hallucinatory voices often insult him and frequently use vile language. That leaves him feeling threatened and fearful, and it also makes it really hard to concentrate on anything else.

Thinking clearly is hard too. His thoughts often seem muddled. Trying to make sense of these disordered perceptions is hard enough, but when his mind is also foggy and confused, it all becomes too much for him, and he often seems not just distracted but as if he is in a world of his own. And in many ways he is.

Even when he is being less affected by those acute symptoms, Ben still lacks initiative and finds it hard to organise himself. As a result, basic tasks like washing, shaving and keeping his clothes clean are often too much for him. His dishevelled state often acts as a barrier between himself and others. Keeping to routines is difficult, and that not only disrupts relationships but has also prevented him from holding down a job.

The disturbance to his thinking and the disorder in his perceptions is unsettling. Smoking helps calm things a little, and he is now close to being a chain smoker. Alcohol definitely takes the edge off his anxieties, and from time to time he's used cannabis and other stronger street drugs to help himself cope.

In calmer times, Ben is keen to engage with church and expresses a clear faith and a definite trust in Jesus. His small group really do care about him and have made involving him in their activities a clear priority, but they, like many others, aren't at all sure how best to help.

Ben and the wider world

Ben has been involved with the mental-health services for nearly a decade now. He has a community psychiatric nurse whom he sees about once a month (and more often than that in the bad times). His visits to the psychiatrist tend to focus on his antipsychotic medication—and he's been tried on many different drugs over the years. The staff on the acute ward know him well because there have been a number of admissions over the years. It can be scary for Ben when his psychotic symptoms are in full flow. And though he would never be able to say it at the time, an admission can sometimes be a kind of relief. It is, in that sense, a kind of asylum. It is certainly a relief to his increasingly elderly parents, for whom an acute phase can be so very disturbing.

In between those acute episodes, Ben's neglect of self-care affects the way he is treated. Those who know him—both at church and in a local support group he attends—are able to overlook his dishevelled state, but in other settings Ben is aware that people are giving him a wide berth, and sometimes he notices people pointing and talking about him. None of that helps his tendency toward paranoid thoughts.

Helping Ben by raising awareness

Over the years there has been a steady growth in the understanding that Ben's church has concerning his struggles. Initially, that centred around his small group. They took it upon themselves to arrange a meeting with a local Christian psychiatrist so that he could provide some background information about schizophrenia and the different impacts it can have upon people. The group leaders followed that up with a visit to meet the leaders of a local charity that ran a support group for people who had been diagnosed with a psychotic illness.

The psychiatrist provided a framework that helped Ben's group orientate themselves at a time soon after the diagnosis when they were all fairly confused. The visit to the support group was particularly helpful in answering practical questions about the best way to support Ben going forward.

These meetings gave the small group confidence to ask the pastor of their church if it might be possible to arrange a church-wide meeting where people could learn about the more serious forms of mental illness. They were careful to respect Ben's privacy, and they avoided any direct reference to Ben or his family. It turned out that several people in the church had personal experience of supporting others with psychotic illnesses. Sometimes this had been in previous churches and sometimes through illnesses which had affected their wider families. This shared experience helped the church see that these kinds of difficulties weren't as unusual as they had thought and also reassured them that the church had people with skills and experience that could be used to support people facing these difficulties.

Helping Ben relate

One of the key things those church meetings achieved was to overcome the fear of the unknown, which had been preventing people from reaching out to Ben. With a clearer sense of what to expect, people found it easier to move toward Ben with simple acts of kindness or conversation. Instead of judging him for his inability to sit still and seeing him as a disruptive influence, people were able to feel and express much greater compassion toward Ben.

Lowering expectations helped too. Once people knew that even a brief interaction could be significant by contributing to a broader sense of Ben's belonging to the church, many more people felt able to engage with Ben on a Sunday.

The small group also revisited the way that they would engage with Ben. Recognising that he found it almost impossible to sit through a long meeting, they agreed an alternative plan. Ben would aim to come to the opening social part of the evening (and people would take it in turns to offer him a lift), and then (provided the weather allowed) someone in the group would generally head out for a walk with Ben before returning to join in with the final time of prayer. They knew that this pattern would be easiest in the longer summer evenings, and would probably need rethinking after a while, but it was good to have a plan to work to.

Ben's small group were aware that Ben longed to be useful to the church, but none of the usual areas of service seemed possible. That led to the suggestion that Ben might come and do some practical work in the church building one morning each week. There was always a need to collect left-over service sheets after the Sunday meetings, and since that could be done at any time on Monday or Tuesday, Ben could come in at a time that suited him. Usually one of the people in the office did the job alongside him, and that usually led to some relaxed conversation as they worked. In a very small way, increasing his regularity in coming in for this task became a way of learning skills that would be needed if he was to try and find a part-time job.

Helping Ben remember his identity

Having a richer sense of his own identity in Christ wasn't something that Ben was ever likely to develop by hours of in-depth Bible study. Ben learnt more about his identity in Christ by first-hand experiences of belonging. When members of the church included him in their activities, when they worked hard to identify gifts he might have and put them to use, Ben felt he belonged. He experienced being a member of the body of Christ. He was never likely to articulate that experience in theological language, but it was being made real for him in relationship. He was, in that sense, experiencing 1 Corinthians 12 being worked out in practice. He wasn't being told, "We don't need you", but as a weaker part of the body he was being treated "with special honour" (1 Corinthians 12:21-23).

Ben also learnt that he was valuable to God through the experience of being valued by God's people. When his church family treated him with love and respect (in ways that weren't reflected in other contexts), Ben learnt about grace and love. The love with which he was being loved reflected the love of Christ and so taught him more about it (1 John 4:11-12).

Helping Ben be refined

The learning and growth that God brought about in Ben was achieved through small steps. One time after collecting all the service sheets from the church building, one of the staff team said, "Isn't it strange how good it is to tidy something up? I think that's because God is a God of order and not chaos." With so much of Ben's life (and his mental processes) feeling chaotic, that idea really struck home. He liked the idea that even if his life felt chaotic, God wasn't.

Another time he was surprised to hear someone in his home group talking about the fear of things being out of control. Not only were they caring for elderly parents, but they had recently been diagnosed with a serious cancer. But they said that they were determined to trust because even if they couldn't understand or control what was happening, God did understand, and God was in control. That simple idea of trust hit home to Ben, and he often remembered it when he too felt afraid because things seemed out of control.

Finally, people close to Ben worked hard to help him notice when he was going downhill. Persuading him to seek and accept help, perhaps with an increase in medication, before it was too late was so important, and learning to trust others was a key part of that.

It wasn't always smooth sailing. Like the time Ben shouted out at the children's nativity service "That's my Mum!" when the girl playing Mary walked in. Or the time he started a passionate and increasingly strange argument with a Jehovah's Witness who made the mistake of knocking on his door. These things were setbacks not just for him but for the confidence of others in him. But in time, they even learned to laugh at these things together, and they became an enjoyable part of the church family story.

Helping Ben with some practical resources

Different people played key roles in helping Ben to establish regular routines. Picking him up for home group or Sunday service or when he was coming in to help in the church building didn't always work, but it created more order than there would have been otherwise.

Ben also needed help with forms and finances. Getting the right allowances meant filling in the right forms, and Ben always needed help there. When a possible job opening came up, people supported him in completing the application form and getting to the interview, and though he didn't get the job, he felt loved.

People also supported Ben by being an advocate. Once when he was picked up by the police for shouting in the shopping mall, it was one of the church leaders who arrived just in time to calm things down and prevent him from being arrested.

At other times people from the church have accompanied Ben to doctor's appointments and supported him when he was exploring some possible new housing options.

The long-term relationships Ben has developed in church and the growing understanding people have of his difficulties make it possible for his church to support him in ways that would never have been possible a few years ago. And what his church friends tell him, but he really doesn't understand at all, is that caring for Ben is good for them. They say it teaches them more about the love of Christ and the importance of church. These are just words to Ben; he can't make sense of what they mean. But he does sense that people say those words with compassion, and that they really do seem to take time with him—and in a way that he really can't describe, that feels good. He feels like he belongs.

CHAPTER 16

CARING FOR THE CARERS

Remember **Kelly**? She's a lovely, godly woman. She's gifted, humble, kind—just the sort of person you want reading the Bible one to one with the younger women around. But she's struggling at home as her youngest teenage daughter seems to be disappearing before her eyes. She doesn't understand why her daughter isn't eating; she can't get her head around the cuts on her daughter's arms. This time last year the family were so happy: mealtimes were a joy, and feelings were shared, not suppressed. But something somewhere broke. Now she feels impotent in the face of her daughter's slow-motion self-destruction. And nothing, either from friends or anyone else, even begins to help.

Understanding Kelly

In this chapter we will consider the difficulties which arise because of struggles with an eating disorder. But our focus won't be on the provision of help to the person struggling with an eating disorder. Instead, we will consider the ways in which a church might support their immediate family— and, in this case, specifically the mother of someone with anorexia.

Caring for carers is a critical component in any consideration of mental-health difficulties. Every prolonged struggle with mental health will bring considerable burdens to close family members. An understandable desire to protect the privacy of their loved one, combined in many cases with a sense of shame, will often leave relatives desperately isolated. No one in their immediate circle of friends may know what they are facing. Or, if they do know, they may still have no idea what to say. Often that fear of saying the wrong thing becomes the reason for saying nothing.

Church, tragically, seems to many people to be the very hardest place to talk. Non-Christian friends often turn out to be more sympathetic and less judgmental than brothers and sisters in the body of Christ. Understanding why that might be, and changing it, is crucial. Only then will our churches become the kind of supportive environment we know they should be.

Kelly is used to being successful. Parenting is something she has enjoyed and from which she has gained considerable satisfaction. So when her daughter Jade began to develop difficulties with eating, Kelly was taken entirely by surprise. For months, she persuaded herself that Jade was just going through a phase and that the fussy eating would soon pass.

But it didn't pass. It intensified. More meals were missed; more food was left on the plate. Sometimes relief at a "successfully eaten meal" was replaced by dismay when Kelly found the discarded food hidden in her daughter's room. Kelly's initial determination not to make a big thing out of it was soon replaced by lengthy interrogations and appeals for change. But those were frustratingly one-way conversations. Jade's sullen attitude and largely monosyllabic replies gave little insight into what was really going on.

Kelly, of course, did her research. She devoured books about anorexia and was dismayed to discover the gloomy statistics associated with the condition. Not only was it the psychiatric illness with the highest mortality, but only 30-40% of people were said to make a full recovery. Others struggled on for years, their whole lives often marred by disordered eating.

After the distress of seeing her daughter struggling so profoundly, the next worst thing was the feeling of guilt and shame. A mother is supposed to feed her child. Parenting functions don't come much more basic than that. And Kelly couldn't do it—she wasn't being allowed to do it. And it was driving her mad. Her husband was no help. He'd checked out ages ago. His angry tirade at the dinner table one day had brought tears from Jade and fury from Kelly. After that he'd said that clearly his help wasn't wanted, so perhaps it was best if he said nothing at all. And he didn't. And doesn't. The gulf between Kelly and her husband is wide and getting wider.

Kelly and the wider world

Church has become increasingly painful. Everyone, Kelly is convinced, must know what is going on. Jade's steady loss of weight is evident for everyone to see. Yet though the problem is, in that sense, public, it still gets ignored. Kelly has this sense that people are talking about her. But they certainly aren't talking to her. No one asks. No one offers to pray. It feels like the great unmentionable.

When Jade starts refusing to join the rest of the family at church, Kelly is almost relieved. She wonders if people at church are too. It makes it easier for them all to pretend. At least Jade's school takes an interest. Jade's form tutor makes contact and observes that Jade seems to be struggling with her weight. It's a relief that someone has finally noticed and said something, but Kelly still finds herself minimising and excusing and speaking vaguely about a phase and things getting better. Jade's teacher doesn't seem convinced but doesn't press. She mentions help that might be available from the child and adolescent mental healthcare system (known as CAMHS in the UK).

It takes another month for Kelly to actually pick up the phone and contact them. They speak of a very long waiting list and make suggestions about a visit to the family doctor. An assessment appointment is promised, but the timing seems uncertain.

Kelly, of course, can't drop everything to focus on Jade. She has a part-time job to keep up. There are two other children to care for, and her own parents are getting increasingly frail. And now her marriage is feeling distinctly fragile. If Jade would just start eating, things would be so much easier. She does get cross sometimes—even though she tries not to show it.

Helping Kelly by raising awareness

As Kelly sees it now, Margaret's arrival still seems something of a miracle. A retired social worker, Margaret had only joined the church relatively recently but had already impressed Kelly as being a caring and wise older woman. She was certainly wise in the way she approached Kelly. No judgments. No presuming to know. Just a gentle introduction, a compassionate enquiry and an offer to meet and talk more.

Margaret, it turned out, had experience in mental health and had even given seminars in her previous church, including one on eating disorders. Kelly was so relieved to finally find someone who could speak about these things without sounding awkward or embarrassed. Margaret thought a seminar for the church would feel far too pointed. They were a small church, and everyone would have a sense why this was happening. But Margaret asked Kelly if she might consider creating a prayer triplet who could commit to praying for Jade and the wider family regularly. If she did, then Margaret could perhaps come and speak with them to help them understand so that they could know how to support Kelly and the family.

And that was the basis for the afternoon they all spent together two weeks later. Kelly had invited two close friends (both of whom, it turned out, had been desperate to help but couldn't work out how to), and Margaret joined them to provide some background information.

They learnt so much that afternoon. But perhaps the biggest help was discovering that there seem to be a whole range of factors that may contribute to the development of anorexia. Our shape-obsessed culture does play a part, but so do genes, and stress, and personality, and peer pressure and much else besides. Kelly's sense that it was all her fault began to ease a little. She's always assumed that if only she'd been a better mother this would never have happened, but hearing Margaret's explanations changed that. Knowing her friends had heard the same things made it so much easier to talk to them. She felt less defensive, less judged, and definitely less alone.

Helping Kelly relate

From that point on the prayer triplet became a lifeline. They met weekly and set to praying not just for Jade but for every part of the situation and family. Kelly felt supported and cared about for the first time in months. Being able to talk about it in the company of her newly understanding friends made it easier to talk about in other contexts as well.

Margaret had directed Kelly to a support website used by parents. On its chat forum she discovered just how common her own experience was. One of the key things she discovered was just how often marriages struggle in these situations. That gave her confidence to move toward her husband and open up conversations with him. There was information on the website specifically written by fathers with experience of having a daughter with anorexia. Her husband found those articles really enlightening, and, even if it didn't remove all the differences in their approach, it certainly got them talking again.

Together they approached their pastor to seek his advice and wisdom. The very first thing he did was apologise for not having reached out to them. Before speaking with Kelly, Margaret had approached their pastor. She had wanted to make sure that any input she offered had his approval and wasn't going to be clashing with anything else that was going on. The pastor had acknowledged his ignorance and had, since then, read enough about eating disorders to realise how inadequate the church's response had been. He knew he wasn't in a position to offer specific guidance but wanted to provide more general support in terms of prayer and in encouraging Kelly and her husband to make good use of whatever support networks they could. That included agreeing what would be said to their small-group leaders and to Jade's youth-group leaders.

It turned out that the leaders in Jade's youth group had been worrying about her for some time but, like everyone else, had felt paralysed. It was a relief to them too that the issue was finally out in the open. They were only too glad to meet up with Kelly and her husband to work out how communication with them would both respect Jade's privacy and provide appropriate reassurance to Jade's parents.

Helping Kelly remember her identity

Ongoing conversations with Margaret proved very helpful to Kelly in understanding some of the ways in which she had reacted to this whole situation. Being a "successful" parent had mattered hugely to Kelly. Jade had, in all sorts of ways, been her model child. Jade was academically strong and had set incredibly high standards for herself. Looking back, Kelly could see that she had rather liked that. Without realising it, Kelly had tended to see Jade's successes as evidence of her own parenting achievements. Instead of giving thanks to God for blessings in Jade's life, she had ended up mentally patting herself on the back.

There was, of course, nothing wrong about Kelly wanting to be a good parent. But what she came to see was how much her motivation mattered. Loving her children for God's sake and to honour him was so very different to loving them so that she could feel good about her own achievements.

A more measured view of successes and failures was a help too. Revisiting the Bible's teaching about the sinful nature and the Spirit reminded her that every believer was a complicated mix of good and bad. She read one really helpful article that described the Christian as saint, sufferer and sinner. Every Christian believer is simultaneously a person in whom God is at work—that is, a saint indwelt by God's Spirit; a person impacted by the difficulties and demands of a fallen world—that is, a sufferer who knows trouble; and a person whose own heart is still tugged toward false desires and false gods—that is, a sinner whose heart continues to deceive them. Seeing herself and Jade in those terms provided a much better perspective on what kinds of things they both needed.

Helping Kelly be refined

It would be wrong to suggest that Kelly's heart was transformed overnight or that the lessons she was learning didn't sometimes feel distinctly shaky. But gradually certain things were becoming clearer. First of all, she came to realise that she didn't like feeling vulnerable and she didn't like asking for help. That had certainly got in the way of her talking with friends. She saw now that the reason why her friends struggled to talk with her about Jade wasn't simply about their own reluctance. Kelly was also sending some pretty loud messages about not wanting anyone's help.

That independent streak also extended to her relationship with God. She was, of course, praying for God's help, but there was a certain lack of humility and a lack of real dependence in those prayers. Gradually she was coming to see that.

Control was an intriguing issue too. Kelly wanted her daughter to eat. Of course she did. And her inability to control her daughter's behaviour in this regard was maddening. But then again, control was what her daughter was doing lots of. Controlling her weight, certainly. But controlling their family too. And all of this took place against the backdrop of Kelly's theological conviction that it is God who is really in control. Of course such a truth isn't without its complexities, in times of suffering most of all. But knowing that God was finally in control and could be trusted, even in hardship, really was beginning to be so important to her.

2 Corinthians had been a place where she had camped out for some time in her Bible-reading. Its exploration of the themes of weakness and power had given her lots to reflect on. Job helped too. Sometimes Kelly felt assaulted by difficulties, and Job's closing confrontation with the greatness of God certainly helped her perspective.

Helping Kelly with some practical resources

Expert advice had been important from the word go. Margaret had given Kelly books written by other Christian parents, and even if she didn't agree with all that they had written, those accounts were a vital first step in reducing Kelly's sense of isolation. Website articles focusing on the experience of parenting a child with anorexia were a very specific help, and so was an account by a woman who had been through a long period of anorexia herself. That account really helped Kelly grow in understanding of her daughter.

When the appointment at CAMHS did eventually come through, they too had plenty of resources to offer, and she wondered if, perhaps, she could have got them earlier if only she had asked.

More broadly, the church had provided important support to help certain normal things to keep happening. Practical care in the form of sleepovers and childcare made it possible for Kelly and her husband to get a much-needed weekend away to recharge. That was only possible because those who provided support for Jade that weekend were sufficiently in the loop. Jade would never have accepted it otherwise.

What also mattered was the persistence of that help. It was clear to Kelly that Jade's struggles with eating weren't going away any time soon. The fact that support from her church family, and especially her prayer triplet, also showed no sign of letting up mattered more than she could say.

WHY WE WROTE THIS BOOK

Both of us care passionately about those who struggle with their mental health, and both of us long for our churches to be places where people who struggle in this way will feel welcomed. But it is also our conviction that the calling to care is for the *whole congregation* of God's people, and not just pastoral professionals or specialists. So we wanted to create a resource that encouraged ordinary church members to see how they can play a part in supporting and helping those struggling with their mental health. We hope these chapters have provided prompts toward that goal.

We are, however, very much aware of this book's limitations. Neither of us are currently working as mental-health professionals—which means this is definitely not an up-to-the-minute survey of current thinking in the field. Moreover, this is a relatively short book. We have only dipped our toes into what is a considerable ocean. Much more that could have been said and all sorts of extra information might have been helpful. But when so little has been written specifically to help churches respond well to mental-health needs, we hope this can be a start.

We need to repeat: this book won't equip you for every situation. It won't make anyone an expert. But we do hope it will encourage some of you who read it to move *toward* those who struggle when previously you might have moved *away*. We also hope it might enable some people to persevere with their friends when previously they might have run out of things to say or to do. We hope it might shift the culture in our churches. Where there might previously have been an unspoken "us and them" attitude, we pray that it might increasingly be replaced with a sense of us all being united in our need of a Saviour, whatever form our neediness takes.

In our spiritual need, Christ reaches out to us with the comfort only he can bring. Both of us know first-hand the profound difficulties that mental ill-health can bring. Our longing, as those who have received comfort in Christ, is that God might enable us to build church communities who care really well for those whose mental-health struggles put them in need of comfort.

> *Praise be to the God and Father of our Lord Jesus Christ, the Father of compassion and the God of all comfort, who comforts us in all our troubles, so that we can comfort those in any trouble with the comfort we ourselves receive from God.* 2 Corinthians 1:3-4

FURTHER RESOURCES

This book has given an introduction to the church's role in supporting those who are struggling with their mental health. If you would like to investigate this area in more depth, these resources may provide useful next steps:

Websites
- biblicalcounselling.org.uk
- biblicalcounselingcoalition.org
- CCEF.org
- mindandsoulfoundation.org

Courses
- Certificate in Biblical Counselling from Biblical Counselling UK; www.biblicalcounselling.org.uk
- Pastoral Care Foundations course from Crosslands Training; www.crosslands.training

Devotionals
- *31-Day Devotionals for Life* series (P&R)
- *Hope When It Hurts* by Kristen Wetherell and Sarah Walton (The Good Book Company, 2017)

Books
- *A New Day* by Emma Scrivener (IVP, 2017)
- *Descriptions and Prescriptions: A Biblical Perspective on Psychiatric Diagnoses and Medication* by Michael Emlet (New Growth Press, 2017)
- *Tackling Mental Illness Together: A Biblical and Practical Approach* by Alan Thomas (IVP, 2017)
- *Safe and Sound: Standing Firm in Spiritual Battles* by David Powlison (New Growth Press, 2019). Gives

clear, balanced, biblical and insightful help on the subjects of spiritual warfare and demonic possession.

Addiction
- *Addictions: A Banquet in the Grave* by Edward Welch (P&R, 2001)
- *Crossroads: A Step-by-Step Guide Away from Addictions* by Edward Welch (New Growth Press, 2008)

Anxiety
- *Running Scared: Fear, Worry, and the God of Rest* by Edward Welch (New Growth Press, 2007)
- *Hope in an Anxious World* by Helen Thorne (The Good Book Company, 2021)
- *Living without worry* by Tim Lane (The Good Book Company, 2022)
- *Stress: The Path to Peace* by Simon Vibert (IVP, 2014)

Depression
- *Depression: Looking Up from the Stubborn Darkness* by Edward Welch (New Growth Press, 2011)
- *Down, Not Out: Depression, Anxiety and the Difference Jesus Makes* by Chris Cipollone (The Good Book Company, 2018)
- *When Darkness Seems My Closest Friend* by Mark Meynell (IVP, 2018)

The biblical process of change
- *Real Change: Becoming More Like Jesus in Everyday Life* by Andrew Nicholls and Helen Thorne (New Growth Press, 2018)
- *How People Change* by Tim Lane and Paul Tripp (New Growth Press, 2007)
- *You Can Change* by Tim Chester (IVP, 2008)

Pastoral care in the local church

- *Caring for one another—8 ways to cultivate meaningful relationships* by Edward Welch (Crossway, 2018)
- *Speaking truth in love—Counsel in community* by David Powlison (Evangelical Press, 2008)
- *Instruments in the redeemer's hands* by Paul David Tripp (P&R, 2006)

the good book

C O M P A N Y

BIBLICAL | RELEVANT | ACCESSIBLE

At The Good Book Company, we are dedicated to helping Christians and local churches grow. We believe that God's growth process always starts with hearing clearly what he has said to us through his timeless word—the Bible.

Ever since we opened our doors in 1991, we have been striving to produce Bible-based resources that bring glory to God. We have grown to become an international provider of user-friendly resources to the Christian community, with believers of all backgrounds and denominations using our books, Bible studies, devotionals, evangelistic resources, and DVD-based courses.

We want to equip ordinary Christians to live for Christ day by day, and churches to grow in their knowledge of God, their love for one another, and the effectiveness of their outreach.

Call us for a discussion of your needs or visit one of our local websites for more information on the resources and services we provide.

Your friends at The Good Book Company

thegoodbook.com | thegoodbook.co.uk
thegoodbook.com.au | thegoodbook.co.nz
thegoodbook.co.in